DURGA

Kevin Missal wrote his first book at the age of 14, and at 22, the St Stephens graduate was a bestselling author with the first two books in his Kalki series which were runaway successes. Kevin loves fantasy fiction and has always been a fan of mythology. His books have been featured in publications like the *Sunday Guardian*, *The New Indian Express* and *Millennium Post*. He lives in Gurugram and he can be contacted at Kevin.s.missal@gmail.com.

DEVI SERIES

Book 1

DURGA

Kevin Missal

SIMON &
SCHUSTER

London · New York · Sydney · Toronto · New Delhi

First published in India by Simon & Schuster India, 2022

This edition published in 2022

1 3 5 7 9 10 8 6 4 2

Simon & Schuster India
818, Indraprakash Building,
21, Barakhamba Road,
New Delhi 110001

www.simonandschuster.co.in

PB ISBN: 978-93-92099-24-3
eBook ISBN: 978-93-92099-25-0

Typeset in India by SÜRYA, New Delhi
Printed and bound in India by Replika Press Pvt. Ltd.

FSC
www.fsc.org
MIX
Paper from responsible sources
FSC® C016779

Simon & Schuster India is committed to sourcing paper that is made from wood grown in sustainable forests and support the Forest Stewardship Council, the leading international forest certification organisation. Our books displaying the FSC logo are printed on FSC certified paper.

AUTHOR'S NOTE

What you read here is my utmost tribute to Durga maa. I have read as many versions of the legend as I could, be it from the Markandeya Purana or the Devi Mahatamya and so on.

Please be aware that this not an accurate version at all. This is *my* take on Durga maa's legend. I do not want to falsely claim that any of this is real. It is purely fictitious. I know this story cannot possibly exist since it has stemmed from a single author's mind, but this is a way to show my love and respect to Durga maa and the ones who follow her. What you read further is a mixture of history, mythology and a lot of my imagination.

History Till Now...

Jambudvipa is the land of Jambus. They are little cherry-coloured fruits that are found in each direction of the country. Of course, Jambudvipa became Hindustan and then India as we know it today. But during that time, Jambudvipa was a developing country.

There were tribes. Hundreds of them. All living the most nomadic lifestyle, practising animal husbandry and pastoralism. This was the Early Vedic Age, around 1500 BCE, and this was before the *Ramayana* and the Battle of Ten Kings. In fact, this was the time when kings didn't exist and there was no particular way of living. There was only survival.

When the Rigveda, one of the oldest of the country, came into being, people began to follow it. They began to live according to its principles. And one of the first supporters of these scriptures were the Aryas. They were northern tribesmen.

Once they got enamoured by the Rigveda, they incorporated its teachings into their system, forming a cohesive kingdom in the north. They had priest kings who would worship the elements of nature—fire, water, air and earth. They began to give each other titles like Indra, Varuna, Yama and soon referred to themselves as gods or Devas. And they also began to indulge themselves in yagnas and rituals around somas, drinks that they made from nature. These drinks would give them a soothing sensation and made them feel like they were a part of nature. Those who overindulged in soma came to be known as Suras, which was also what soma was known as.

There were another lot of tribesmen who lived alongside and weren't so affiliated with the Rigveda. They were called Dasas. In fact, they didn't want to follow it or perhaps didn't have the knowledge or will to do so. They remained as they were and lived their lives, while the north flourished and became a massive empire. And then the north began to threaten the south.

The Aryas wanted to form an alliance with the Dasas and the Dasas rejected, not wanting to partake in the drinking of soma and the intoxication it caused. They liked being nomadic and staying away from any sort of disturbance. They liked following their ways of life. The Aryas thus termed them Asuras, opposite to them. With time, the word Asuras took on demonic connotations even though Dasas were humans. Like you. Like me.

While Aryas continued to force themselves on Dasas, one of the Dasa rose up to rebel.

And that, my friends, was Mahisha. Better known as Mahishasura.

He was a strategic man. A powerful, valiant warrior who united all of the tribes of Dasas.

Mahisha singlehandedly formed an empire that lead to the destruction of the Aryas and the formation of Dasas as sole rulers.

Our story though begins when Mahisha was at his peak of power and the Aryas were scattered, trying to fight back against him. Mahisha seemed invincible.

Until they found his weakness.

PROLOGUE

Badrikut, east of Himavat mountains

The green man came. And hundreds followed him.

But before she could see him, witness the physical manifestation of chaos, she was busy with her father, living an ideal life.

Today was fun since she would be taught what to do at the farm. But more than that, it was about spending time with her father, who was a kind, generous man.

Shaila was just eight years old, but she was ready to undertake any sort of teaching her father would give her. And while she should have been busy studying in a gurukul, she was here working on a farm, voluntarily. She repaired the fences that would restrict outsiders from coming in rather clumsily, since it was her first time. She reared the sheep and helped her father to milk the cows. And she had to do all of it when the snow was tough to walk on and everything was wintery and white and pale. There was no sun to be seen, and in the distance the snow-capped hills stood like demigods looming over them.

'It's an art,' he smiled, as he pressed the breasts of the cow. 'You have to do it with the right pressure, so it won't trouble her.'

'Why do we drink from a cow?' Shaila asked.

'Because cows are sacred and their milk gives us strength.'

He was wearing thick furs and oilskins around his body and a cap that shielded his head. So did Shaila, who was wrapped up quite nicely by her mother, who was cooking some brussel sprouts and cauliflower soup.

They lived in the corner of a village by the mountains, a small village that one could easily miss if they weren't looking properly. It was right by a frozen river that now had an icy blue coating and Shaila was prohibited to walk on it. She was told the ice was very shaky and could break if pressure was put on it.

'Tvastr!' cried a voice.

Shaila turned and so did her father, breaking their concentration from the cow to see another villager who was waving at them from outside the fence. She held her hand and walked with her father towards the person.

'How are you?' the man asked.

'Good, good, you?'

'Ah, well.'

They shared the niceties while Shaila watched them with a crooked eye as a blearing light hit her face. In the village, everyone knew each other and Shaila had seen this man, he was a beggar of sorts. But her father would never distinguish between a beggar and a trader, who came every fortnight to buy their expensive milk.

'Can I have a jug of um...?' the man asked nervously.

Her father had an impassive, tight face with blue, striking eyes that Shaila had adopted when she was born.

Shaila didn't know why her father would want to even entertain people like them, people who had nothing to barter with, but came to beg. But she also knew her father wouldn't say no. He never said no.

'Sure,' he smiled. 'I'll just get it.'

As he was moving, the man turned to Shaila and smiled. 'How do you do today, Shaila?'

She didn't answer. Her father had brought the jug and handed it over to the man. He flushed red with happiness and gratitude which was a rare up so high in the world where people were usually pale.

'I'll be on my way then, Tvastr. You are a good man...'

Blood sprayed.

Copius amounts of blood just oozed and dripped on the earth, as the man fell to the ground.

For a moment, Shaila and her father remained as frozen as the snow, confused. Then they saw it. An obsidian bladed arrow inside the thick skull of the man.

Her father grabbed hold of Shaila, tugging her tightly against his chest, leaving a little room for her to see in the back of their farmstead. He began to survey where it had come from, when she saw him through her peripheral vision.

The green man of chaos. And his men, who followed him.

Behind him was a trail of blood. Smoke billowed from the village. One couldn't see much as Shaila's farm was at a distance from the main village, but the havoc that the green man and his group had managed to wreak was evident.

All of them wore heavy armoury, their chests adorned with breastplates. They carried flags that had a buffalo motif made on it.

The man stood tall, deep blotches of green crisscrossing over his face, making it look diseased. Deep brown eyes sat stonily in their sockets, and his long, matted hair was twisted around a string. He had a weapon in his hand. An axe as large as him. And his crown...

The crown.

It had real buffalo horns that rose in a curved fashion on either side and it looked as if he could attack anyone with them. They were glistening in the dark.

'I have always despised poverty and begging,' the man said, his hands folded in front of his chest. He had reached the fence and he could have easily trespassed, but he remained put. His soldiers eyed Shaila. 'Don't you, Tvastr?'

Tvastr knew who he was. He had heard about him. The man who was slowly conquering cities that belong to the Aryas. But he never believed that this man would come here, to such a small vilage.

Shaking, he held Shaila a little too tight. Shaila felt suffocated but she dared not protest. In the icy cold, she could feel heat radiating from her father's body.

'I am Mahisha,' he smiled. He had a very callous, unnatural smile. 'I am your new king.' Shaila could see that these men were wounded and were probably returning from a battle up north.

'The Devas...'

'You don't have to worry about them,' he smiled.

'How do you know my name?'

'Well, you supply the best milk in the north, my friend,' Mahisha said. 'And me and my men get thirsty.

You handle the best cows and feed them well. Take care of them.'

Tvastr didn't say anything. But he was shivering. Alas, not because of the cold.

So Mahisha did. He broke the silence. 'When I was a farmer myself, my mother used to give me milk every day. I got used to it. And when I burnt down that village, and killed the cows, and began my crusade, I wondered if I would ever get milk again until I finally managed to infiltrate an enemy camp and kill each one of their members and capture their cows. I saw they had jugs of milk which I tasted, and I just got so nostalgic. So, I asked a prisoner of war, where they got the milk from and he named you.'

Shaila arched her brows. She knew her father was famous.

'We do not want to force you. Thus, we will continue to stand outside your fence while you will get us jugs of milk.'

'I only have a few gallons. It won't feed your army.'

'Then squeeze your cows till they die. I don't care,' Mahisha thundered.

Her father turned to see the smoky, burnt-down village of his. 'Why did you kill them?'

Mahisha shrugged. 'They were interfering. We will be on our way once you give us the milk and no one else will get hurt.'

Her father remained frozen. By then, Shaila's mother had come out and she asked what was going on, only to see Mahisha when he called out:

'Oh, what a beautiful wife you have, and a daughter who has such pretty eyes.'

The woman was confused. They were all silent.

Shaila watched the green man. He had a lascivious smile on his face.

'Give him the milk, papa,' she said.

'Do what your daughter tells you, Tvastr. Our patience only holds on for a short time.'

Shaila's father looked confused. He wanted to get rid of them, but he didn't want to dry the cows out. They gave the best milk because they were handled and cared for well.

'No,' he said.

'Papa?'

Mahisha raised his brows. He was still grinning, as if he was enjoying this.

Shaila knew of the many virtues her father had—one of them was bravery. But it was also his greatest vice.

'I won't give you the milk,' he said. 'I do not get bullied. I have built this farm from the ground up.'

Mahisha nodded, 'I respect that.'

A smile widening on an already smiling face. 'I always respect a good, strong opposition.'

Her father and mother were forced to walk to the middle of the frozen river, while Mahisha restrained a wailing, screaming Shaila, his thick hands on her shoulders.

Her parents were trying to find balance on the delicate layer of ice on the river, as Mahisha looked on and laughed.

His men, meanwhile, were milking the cows and

any cow that proved to be a problem was gutted and kept aside for roasting at a later time on their downward journey. They didn't care about the cows like her father did.

Her eyes were moist.

'Please, please...' she begged Mahisha, hitting him with her small arms, but she had no effect on him. 'Leave my father.'

Mahisha loomed over her ominously, just like the mountains, and watched her parents.

'It's funny what bravery brings you. I always feel doing the right thing can lead you to more trouble than doing the wrong, Tvastr,' he shouted, so her father could hear him, but Tvastr was too busy concentrating on the ice. 'You should have been smart and made sure your family survived. Now, unfortunately, you have sentenced them to die.'

But her father wasn't listening to Mahisha. He was looking at Shaila.

And he was smiling at her. The weak, pitiless, smile as he mouthed to her:

I love you.

The ice broke. Her parents fell through it.

Shaila's heart went still. She could feel her chest getting heavy as she saw her parents cry and wail from the depths of the frozen water.

'Well then,' Mahisha chuckled, and so did his men, who had by now killed all the cows and had collected as much milk as they could.

Shaila wanted to run. And she did. She didn't wait. She shoved Mahisha's thick arm, biting into it as hard as she could, and ran for her parents. She trudged hastily on the ice. The thin layer of ice on the river began to crack under her steps as she finally reached the hole through which her parents had fallen. She leaned forward and looked inside. She couldn't see anyone. She couldn't see anything but water.

Then she heard the men speak from afar.

'Should we kill the girl?' one of Mahisha's men asked.

Shaila turned to see Mahisha. He was contemplating.

'She can't return to the shore without freezing to death,' he said, referring to the trail of broken ice that she had left behind. She had to swim back now, because the ice would surely give way under her weight if she tried to walk back again, and she knew she couldn't. She was lightly clutching on to the hope that the frozen ice she was lying on wouldn't break. 'And our job is done here. Let's leave. We have a long way to go.'

Soon, the green man and his men became dots.

And she remained there.

For how long, she had no idea.

But she knew she had to get to the shore, even if meant she had to swim there. She had to take the risk.

Her parents were dead and the reality of it was stuck in the form of bile at the back of her throat.

She swallowed it. And she leapt inside the water without a second thought, letting the deep, dark cold seep into her. Shaila could feel her strength ebb away.

I won't survive this.

Twelve years later...

1

Maisuru (modern day Mysore), 1450 BCE

Mahisha lay naked amidst women in a pool of crystal blue water.

His thick arms flexed and tightened, veins popping up while he casually leaned back, relaxing and observing the fifty-feet high ceiling which had strange, ornate designs his architect had made.

Women lapped around him. They kissed him, caressed his cheeks. His mouth. His scarred chest. They giggled. There were five of them.

He had carved out a pool for himself in his royal hall and he should have been enjoying every bit of that, but he was too busy pondering on the days that were yet to come. Defining days, as he was about to make something really important happen for Jambudvipa.

'Might we ask you something, my lord?' One of the women spoke up.

This time Mahisha didn't bother to even look at which one it was. He just nodded mundanely.

'Why is your skin... green?' the girl asked.

Mahisha shot her a sharp look of contempt. He knew he was green. Or a bit of him was. The skin pigmentation condition he was born with was a strange, rare defect. The village doctor, a bhisak, had told his parents he was smalnutritional. Would die any time.

But he survived. For some reason, he did. But the skin colour remained the same, splotches of forest green just here and there, acting as instruments of insecurity.

'What did you just ask me?' he said, in a calm, soothing voice.

The girl was frightened. Her pupils dilated. 'I didn't mean anything.'

Mahisha knew that the insecurity he felt because of his skin colour wasn't public knowledge. For them, his skin colour was...well...war paint or just something he did purposefully. 'No, you meant something, girl.'

'I was...I was just curious.'

At that, everyone in the pool went quiet. Complete silence. They weren't touching him anymore. Only the little waves of the pool were heard.

'Curious?' he smiled.

The girl did smile back. 'Yes.' She was feeling weak, he noticed.

'No, I get it,' he nodded to himself. 'How one could be curious. Don't fret. I am not angry with you, girl.'

The girl was confused about whether to believe him or not. But he was just plain smiling. And regardless of his skin colour, Mahisha was a handsome man. In his late thirties, he had shoulder length hair which was jet black in colour. Irises were brown as a bark of an ancient grove. A jawline that could cut wood in two.

'All right,' she said, coming close to him while the other girls began to giggle again, filling up the silence which had fallen earlier. 'I apologise if I was out of line.'

He shook his head. 'No point.'

'What?'

'No point in apologising.'

With a quick jab of his elbow, he slammed into her teeth and plunged her head inside the pool. The girl began to struggle. He continued to push her teeth in. The water started to become crimson. The other girls scrambled out of the pool, still naked.

The woman thrashed against Mahisha's thick arms and strong grip. But she couldn't do it for long.

In a few moments, she stopped moving.

He left her, a placid expression on his face as he shoved her in the corner of the pool, where she floated up with her face down in the water.

'Whore,' he sighed, as he watched the other women, who had fled to the corners of the room to hide from him.

He was in no mood to kill them. It was a waste to kill without reason, even though women in general often irked him.

But they were also his distractions. Good at making him forget about troubles and just gratifying him. They were objects of desire.

There was a harsh knock on the doors and while he wished it wasn't his soldiers, the doors opened as if the man beyond them didn't care to wait for his summons.

If it had been anyone else, Mahisha would have beheaded the person, but it was his guru. The man behind his success.

Shukr. A guru, a preceptor and a priest. The purohit of his capital. He was a tactical genius.

Shukr was an old man. Scrawny. Lanky. The robe he had on looked like it was wearing him and not the other way round. His hair was white, and there were grey blotches on his papery-white, frozen skin. He was crouching.

He was about to speak, when he saw the dead woman in the pool.

'Why?' he asked with a frustrated grimace.

Mahisha shrugged. 'Does it matter?'

He pulled himself out of the pool and came to his feet. When he clapped his hands, the frightened women who were hiding in the corner came with sheets of cloth and began to wipe him dry. Each of them, afraid to the core, remained professional as they knew that if they didn't listen to him, he would kill them too. 'What is so important?'

'We have a problem,' Shukr said.

'Can it wait? I'm leaving for the borders tomorrow. Let me return.'

Shukr shook his head. 'We need your input first and then you can leave.'

Mahisha could see the impassive face of the old man and he knew he meant something serious. Otherwise, he wouldn't be here.

'Let's go then.'

2

Mahisha wore his girdle over his loins. A sheathed blade hung from it. From his ears hung bangles and he wore a crown. He was, after all, a king. A blue shawl was wrapped diagonally across his chest, exposing one bulky half of it, and on his feet he wore wooden sandals.

He walked behind Shukr, passing through the baked clay corridors of his palace. He was a tall man, towering over most of his soldiers, standing as tall as a giant at almost seven feet. People would be afraid whenever he stepped into the battlefield, he would be the tallest one. There was a myth—without any weapons, he was capable of towing down an elephant. However, this myth was manufactured by Mahisha himself.

He entered a large room, one that had a huge balcony overlooking the entire city, glittering with diyas. This was the war room. Here is where they strategised. There were cushions and sheets on the floor for people to sit on. In the middle stood an elevated wooden platform with the map of Jambudvipa and wooden figurines on it.

As he entered, he saw two other people in the room.

One was Tamra. The Prime Minister of his capital. The levelheaded man with a purple wrapping around his short, thin body. He was a wise person and handled the day-to-day affairs. He had short hair, and over it he wore a ruby-studded headpiece made of gold filigree. And he smelled of lavender.

'What have you rubbed on yourself, you idiot?' Mahisha chuckled, as he laid himself on the cushion. He sought a basket of fruits for himself, and when he found one, kept in the back, he immediately began to savour some grapes.

'It's what my wife gave me,' Tamar smiled, sitting opposite the king.

'Wife? Pfft. Can you believe him?' Mahisha turned to his childhood friend, the second man in the room. Siksh, the Senani of his army. 'I still can't digest he has a wife.'

'Well, he's an independent man,' Siksh said. He had a marble eye instead of his real eye, because he had saved Mahisha from an assassination attempt once and had lost his eye in the process. He was in battle gear; he always was. He was born in it. 'You can't blame him for making a mistake, can you?'

'She's a good woman,' Tamar protested. 'Takes care of the house...'

'Get a bloody slave!' Mahisha snapped.

'She makes me happy.'

'Get a wench then, perhaps?' Siksh suggested.

Tamra sighed. 'You two won't understand what it means to be in love.' He sounded slightly defensive in a gushy and romantic way, something Mahisha would never understand.

Mahisha wanted to retort or say something else, but he refrained. Tamar was a good man compared to Mahisha and Siksh, both of whom would use anger as a weapon the moment they were insulted. Tamar would remain calm and composed, while Mahisha and Siksh would trouble and poke him. Even though they held important positions in the country, they were friends, for they all had started from grassroots to reach where they were today.

'If your fun and games are over, can we talk?' Shukr interjected, not sitting, but circling around them like a teacher.

'Go on, guruji,' Mahisha allowed.

'Great.' From under his thick sleeve, he pulled out a scroll. 'I have had spasas in the entire subcontinent as you know, disguised as ordinary folks, but listening to whispers that could be harmful to the great empire that we have created.'

Spasas? Mahisha knew they were these spy networks that Shukr was really good at managing. He would get updates about the rebels, the Aryas who were a constant threat. It was funny, how once upon a time, they were the rulers of the land. But now he ruled while they were in hiding, hoping to find a way to kill him.

'He had something important to report,' Shukr continued.

'And what's that?' Tamar's brows were drawn together.

'The Aryas have planned a swift attack on us,' Shukr said.

'Attack?' Mahisha snorted. 'They are dying out. They are hidden. What attack can they carry out? Perhaps hit our walls and run away?' He snorted. So did Siksh.

'A smart one, your highness,' Shukr said through gritted teeth. 'Do not be overconfident because of your ego, Mahisha. Remember where you came from.'

Mahisha flared his nostrils. No one would dare to talk to him like this, but Shukr was different, even though right then he wanted to choke his guru for speaking to him like that. But he just clenched his hands into fists and remained frozen.

'Anyway, the Aryas have been planning this attack for quite some time,' he was reading from the scroll and paraphrasing, 'while we were busy expanding our kingdom's foreign networks with the Greeks, Egyptians, and Afghanis. They were creating a perfect weapon.'

'And what weapon might that be?' Siksh asked. 'Is it a ball of fire that will ignite on command? Or perhaps something else? More advanced? How can it be possible that they have this weapon without having the resources, since we have bled them dry from all sides?'

Shukr shook his head. 'The weapon is an assassin.'

Mahisha raised his brow. 'An assassin? I have had multiple attempts made on me, guruji. How is this assassin any different?'

'This assassin has been told to kill you in the next nine days. Tomorrow is day one,' Shukr explained. 'And the worst part is, this assassin is *already* inside our kingdom, hidden and disguised. We don't know the assassin's identity.'

For a moment, they were all quiet.

Then Mahisha said, 'He's a spy?'

'A lethal one. Anda...' he continued to read from the scroll, 'she's a woman.'

Mahisha looked at Siksh and they both burst into laughter, their bodies lurching forward, while Tamar remained quiet, understanding the gravity of the situation.

Mahisha could almost feel his pulse beating with energy as he finished his grapes and came to his feet. 'I should go. I have to prepare myself for tomorrow.'

'What? How are we going to deal with her?' Shukr asked.

'We don't. Guruji,' he said calmly, 'it's a woman. I am sure one woman can't kill me.' He wore his slippers while Siksh got up as well. He too was not taking this meeting seriously. 'When she attacks within the next nine days, we will take over and...well, kill her.'

'You are underestimating her,' Shukr warned. 'The Aryas have been working on her for more than a decade now. There must be something in her, that's why she's being sent. Why would they be so confident about their nine-day theory otherwise?

Mahisha clenched his jaw. 'Because they are stupid, guruji. They had everything and I took it from them. Snatched it. Do you really think," he said, coming close to the old man, towering over him, 'I will lose everything because of a woman? She will not be able to stop me.'

'I still think,' Shukr wasn't afraid of Mahisha's bulkiness, 'you should think of some preventive action.'

Mahisha looked at him indignantly. He wanted to get rid of the old man. Even though he had helped him, Shukr was getting paranoid and becoming a weakness in his future plans for Jambudvipa.

'I will be setting off to Kanchipura to seek an allegiance with the Panas.' He was talking about the tribe of Scythians. 'The allegiance is going to be tough. It will be a long-drawn process. The Panas are the most ruthless, war-mongering tribe out there. If they side with us, our military strengthens. And you want me to leave that and focus on a...what is it? A girl.'

Tamar came in between Mahisha and Shukr, who were shooting looks of contempt at each other and said: 'Your highness, I believe you both are right. Why don't we come to a compromise?'

'And what will that be?' Mahisha asked his friend.

'Siksh and I can figure out who this assassin is, while you go out and make good relations with the Panas,' Tamar offered, while Siksh rolled his eyes at the plan, for he himself wasn't taking it seriously.

Mahisha impassively watched Shukr and then a smile came on his lips. 'I think that works, doesn't it, guruji?'

Shukr nodded weakly. The old man was tired of the enormous ego his pupil had. He wanted them to be like they were back in the gurukul where he used to teach these three how to be the usurpers of power. He had seen passion and hunger for violence in them and had chosen them. But now...they were different. Except for Tamar, who grew up somewhat right, at least.

'It does.'

'Great. Siksh, please make sure this woman is caught and is imprisoned till I return so I can kill her myself. And do your work diligently, so our sweet guruji is pacified that we did take his paranoia seriously.' He said this all through gritted teeth, while Siksh nodded.

'As you say, your highness,' he said in return.

Mahisha left the room, not looking back. They remained as quiet as a mouse, until Siksh spoke up from the corner, breaking that awkward silence left by their king: 'Guruji, does this assassin have a name?'

Shukr nodded again, sighing. It was a small beam of hope; his spasa had got hold of a name too. 'Yes, there is.'

'Great. Tell me, so I can inform my captains about it. They'll keep an eye out for her and ask around, perhaps.'

Shukr read the scroll with a narrowed gaze.

'It's a strange one,' he said, as he finally said the name. 'She goes by the name Durga.'

3

Fifty-two miles from Kaveri river...

She knew she had to kill all of them but one by tonight.

With keen, peering eyes, she watched the outpost of Maisuru, close to Lalithabridu town which was in the south of the capital. The outpost was made of clay and baked red sandstones, yellow bricks, and was a multi-storeyed fort. The gates were made of iron grills, and they were flanked by two guards in flashy battle gear complete with spears and a shield each.

There were diyas in every corner of the fort, providing much-needed light in the blanket of darkness that the earth had succumbed to at this time of night.

The plan starts from here, she thought.

The outposts were used as bastions that guarded the paths that led the enemy to the middle of the city. They were also there to send warnings, if an enemy was seen approaching the city. Huge wooden logs were set aflame and the smoke that would create were used as signals to the other outposts right up to the guard towers of the capital. These forts were on elevations too, so they could see into far off distances with ease.

Concealed deep within the foliage around her, with cat-like eyes, she watched the walls.

Could she jump over them?

She was acrobatic, she knew, but even she had limitations.

She heard two things in a brief five seconds. One was the hoot of an owl, and the other was the growl of a large predator.

She could feel the predator sniffing her clothes. She was wearing a tight dhoti and a long scarf diagonally across her body, covering her bosom and showing a bit of her waist. Her weapon—an iron dagger—was stuffed in the corner of the dhoti. She had no footwear. She needed none.

'Calm down, boy,' she said to the tiger, who after sniffing her, came to her side. 'I know you want to eat all of them. But we need to think straight. We can't let them fire up the logs, otherwise the capital will be...' she said, realizing belatedly that she was talking to an animal and chuckled to herself.

He had been her pet since her childhood, but he was also a wild animal who, on being directed towards a victim, would maul them to death.

'Okay, here's the plan, Dawon...' and she made him understand with the click of her fingers. It was not just the act of clicking that Dawon understood, but also the rhythm and the specific sounds of each click, from which he inferred instructions. If the sound was wrong, the tiger would do something different than what he was trained to do.

She clicked once. *Go to the gate.*

She clicked three times. *Attack.*

She patted the ear. *Withdraw if injured.*

The tiger didn't wait for an approval. He just launched himself forward, aiming for the main gate. She had learnt to use the movement of sounds and touch to tame animals. She had taught the animal to associate a sound with a particular action and when he had learnt it, she would feed the tiger ground beef as a reward. Tigers were intelligent predators and over the years, would catch on to something like this.

Just as her tiger lurched at one of the guards, while the other froze in shock and terror, she made her way to the gate as well.

The guard was about to prod the animal with the spear when she brought the dagger close to him, blindsiding him, and slit his throat from behind. Blood sprayed and he collapsed, while the tiger had mauled the other soldier and was eating his guts.

'Move on, my friend. By the end of it, you can easily have food for eternity, if we do it quickly.'

Dawon groaned and moved deeper into the outpost, roaring. While it wouldn't alarm the guards into calling for reinforcements and informing the capital, it would definitely scare them. Five of the guards began to come towards the tiger. While they were preoccupied, she moved up the stairs and towards the tower, concealing herself in the shadows when need be.

She was quick, but was also worried about Dawon getting hurt. He was, after all, her friend. Her only friend, if she thought about it.

She worked her way to the tower's mouth where she saw a guard, whistling to himself. With a quick plunge of her dagger deep into his spine, and closing his mouth at the same time, she killed him. And life ebbed out of his body. Then she calmly put him down on the ground, a pool of blood forming around him.

She looked at the logs which would have been used to send a signal. Quickly, she began to throw the logs as far as possible outside the tower. There were more than a hundred of them and she would throw as many as she could until her arms got tired. As she was making her way through them, her eyes sharply drew downwards to Dawon.

He had been pierced thrice with the blades. At the hip, the arm and the leg. An instant flurry of concern tightened her throat.

No.

Dawon was not pulling back and she wanted to snap her fingers so that he would do so. She recalled patting him gently earlier to tell him he had to withdraw if injured, but tigers often don't listen if they are in the heat of the action.

Also, she knew, he couldn't escape. The guards had encircled him by now.

She saw the logs and then glanced back at her friend. A decision had to be made. Then she pushed the logs down the stairs. The remaining wooden stumps began to trip and fall, as she stepped on the ledge of the tower.

And she jumped.

Her dagger was clutched horizontally in her teeth when she made the lurch.

If she didn't know how to jump, she wouldn't have. But jumps from heights are often done with precise calculation. Plus, this was the third floor.

She had to just...

She instantly tightened her feet and put pressure on them, lifted her arms, and made her body firm.

And when she landed, she could feel the ground taper off that energy and wither that firmness, but she didn't fall, for her jump was perfect.

The dust swirled around her when she did it and the guards, whose attention was on Dawon, turned to her.

'Who are...'

They couldn't speak further, for this distraction was all that Dawon needed. He instantly clawed two of them, and bit into someone else.

Two guards moved for her.

She took the dagger from her mouth and braced herself. As they closed in, she crouched and rolled over, her back pressing against the pebbles. Swiftly, she sliced the veins of the calf of one soldier. And with her legs, she kicked the other one down.

Dawon shrieked in pain and her heart galloped with tension. She turned to see that a huge spear had struck her tiger in the chest and he had fallen to the ground. The guard was being ruthless.

And as she moved to save him, the guard she had kicked, jumped on her back and she fell on the ground too.

He brought the sword next to her throat.

For a moment, her and Dawon's eyes met. They were of different species, but they were connected deeply. She could see Dawon was in excruciating pain.

Then she clicked the inside of her tongue, to make a sound which meant:

One last attack. You can do it.

Dawon growled and with a quick, sweeping slash of his claws, plunged into the spear-holding guard's chest. The guard fell dead, bleeding out. Alas, Dawon remained on the ground, unmoving because the spear was still in him.

I hope he'll be fine.

The blade next to her throat came closer and she knew he was going to kill her, slit her throat, when she…

Bit into the arm of the guard, till she could taste his salty blood and his disgusting flesh.

He screamed, his blade loosening around her neck. She used that moment to roll over with force, making the guard on her back fall on the side.

She came to her feet and the first thing she did was race towards Dawon and kneel next to him.

'Should I pull it out?' she asked.

He growled.

She nodded, bringing her hands around the thick wooden shaft of the spear. With a sharp yank, she pulled it out. Dawon roared in agony and then made a sound like a mewling cat. She tossed the spear to the side, next to the mauled corpses, to inspect the damage done. The wound was deep and ghastly.

But not irreparable. Dawon suffered worse during practices and he would often get up and behave like nothing had happened.

'You'll be fine. A day or two of rest is all you need. I'll get you the ayurveda medicines.' She knew these outposts held infirmaries with pain-numbing medicines. 'But for now…' she tore a large strip off the lower part of her dhoti and tied it around the wound to stop the bleeding. 'Just don't move this.'

Dawon growled softly and she patted him on the head.

'I told you to retreat if you get hurt.'

But she saw her friend being reluctant and stubborn before resting his head back on the ground. The bright orange and white colours of his skin mixed with the crimson blood.

She walked back to the guard who was flailing on the ground and trying to move for the exit of the outpost. She casually walked towards him, and with a quick jab at his arm, pinned him to the ground.

'Don't kill me...don't kill me...'

He was the last of them. Dawon had killed several of the guards and she did as well.

'I won't. Because you are my messenger,' she knelt down. 'And all of this...' she confidently showed all the corpses of the guards, '...is my message, a way to attract attention.'

'Wh-wh-what do you need?'

'Seek General Seksh in the capital. No one else.'

There was fear in his eyes. His bronze helmet was lopsidedly hanging from his head.

'And tell him to come here. To this outpost.'

'W-w-why?'

'To capture me, of course.'

He was confused. Capture? 'W-w-who are you?'

'Durga,' she paused. 'He will know who I am.'

4

She woke up with a gasp.

But her body didn't. It was paralysed on the bed, and she could feel her arms and legs glued to the mattress. She tried to pull away, but the only thing she could move was her face. She was not able to speak.

And then she saw them.

They had come. All the kids. They were laughing. They were pointing fingers. They had familiar faces.

No...no...they aren't real, she cried to herself.

'PRETA! PRETA!' they called her.

She was a ghost, they said. She was white like a ghost.

But it was not her problem. It was the way she was born. Extremely white and with wide, glittering red eyes. She was called a natural-born monster by the kids.

And even though she was twenty years old, they were pointing at her. The kids. They laughed. They picked at her nose. They slapped her.

And then she found herself dissolving. Into pure, dark mud. She was pushed and shoved by these kids inside the mud which was once her mattress. Darkness was enveloping her.

She was dirty. She was stinking.

She accidentally swallowed the dirt and choked on it, when she heard a familiar voice call out:

'GAURI!'

'GAURI!'

She could feel someone else's hands shaking her.

And she woke up.

For a moment, she just counted her breath. She watched the blank ceiling. Her face was sweaty. She tried to move her arms and legs, relieved when she was able to do it. Her breathing steadied, and a sigh broke through her. A smile caught on her face.

I'm alive. It's all just a nightmare.

'Are you okay, Gauri?' the voice beckoned her into the present.

It was her friend, with whom she shared a small quarter. Her name was Airavati and she was watching her with wide, worried eyes, her hands on Gauri's chest.

'Yeah. Yeah, I am, uh...'

'I saw you were struggling again. Shivering and trying to move.'

'Thanks for waking me up.'

'Nightmare?'

Gauri straightened herself and leaned back against the wall. 'Yeah,' she replied in a small voice.

Airavati wouldn't ask what it was; she knew Gauri would never tell her.

But it was the nightmare from her childhood. From when she was eight years old and was pushed down in a swamp by her bullies. It was traumatic, to say the least.

'Don't move.'

'What?'

'Don't move,' Gauri said.

'What happened?' Airavati flashed her a sharp look of worry.

Gauri's hand slowly moved for the top of Airavati's head, to place it next to the creature, that walked onto her fingers. She didn't hurt the creature, but kept it cupped in her hand.

'What was it?' Airavati was confused.

'An arachnid,' Gauri responded, showing her the eight-legged, palm-sized spider.

'What...' she went white, 'was this on my head?'

'Yeah.'

'Don't mind if I faint.'

Gauri chuckled even though Airavati found no mirth in the situation. But Gauri was always comfortable with insects of all kinds. In fact, she had a strange affinity for them. They were odd and uniquely beautiful. Caterpillars, bugs, spiders, and what not. They all were different.

Perhaps the peculiarity in these creatures made her feel drawn towards them, given she was always treated as a strange, ugly woman, her entire life.

Gauri's job was as simple as it could be. In the strictest terms, she was a servant. She would run around the palace that belonged to King Mahisha and wipe his rooms, clean the clothes, sweep the floors, and cook food for the soldiers and ministers who had found quarters in the multiple rooms of the palace. There were twenty more girls like her, who would do different quarters and parts of the palace. But she wasn't just a cleaner. She was also part of the rituals, helping her employer and the head priest, Shukr, with the daily chores.

Her job was limited to the palace, but she worked within the boundaries of it, the gate, the lawns, and the backyard field.

The palace was inside Mahishapur, which was the capital of Maisuru. Sure, there were districts around Mahishapur like Chamarajnagar, Chikmagalur and Coorg, only to name a few, and they all had their specific functions. Mahisha wouldn't travel to these places often, but people would often come to visit him from the districts to inform him that they were running in the most perfect conditions. He would have his commanders stationed there and forts close to the districts were established as a way to keep a close check. In fact, he would hardly go out, staying within the confines of his kingdom which he narcissistically titled Mahishapur.

And so, it was surprising when all the servants were addressed by the hunched Shukr, informing them that King Mahisha had gone out on an important business excursion.

However, it was not surprising for Gauri at all. She had known of it for quite some time. She had heard about the ravaging Panas who wore iron skull masks and rode on their mammoth horses. Some called them the mythical Kimpurushas who were a hybrid horse-human species. But that was not so. All lies, Gauri knew. Tall tales.

Shukr halted in front of Gauri. 'You need to be in the meeting which we have with the emissary.' He had a throaty voice, as if there was some phlegm he wanted to perpetually get rid of but couldn't. He instructed Airavati to be there too.

It was odd for a purohit to instruct slaves, but Shukr was the spine of the capital. He was compulsive and particular about how things should run, not letting anyone else speak on his behalf—whether it was state affairs or the religious order. And for now, this meeting with the emissary was state-related business.

Gauri thought of this one temple which Shukr often used to live in where the female slaves weren't allowed. In fact, no women were. Only men could go in.

If Gauri ever wanted to enter a temple, it would be that one. To just irk the administrators of the system. Just to irk Shukr.

The meeting was going well—there was laughter and wine, and oranges were being peeled. Whenever Shukr would snap his fingers, Gauri would have to come and serve the basket of fruits with a forced smile, while Airavati would act as a makeshift table on which the wine goblets were placed. There were scribes with wooden tables sitting with leaves and an inked quill.

Gauri could see that her friend was tearing up as her hands and legs were hurting. She couldn't move—if she did, the goblets would fall and she'd be flogged.

Gauri couldn't feel anything but angry and humiliated on her friend's behalf. She wanted to help Airavati, but her hands were tied by the four guards wearing heavy armour and helmets, and they just watched the meeting unfold, standing in the four corners of the room.

Gauri noticed the dark-skinned emissary who was

wearing a funny hat and multicoloured robes. She knew from his accent that he was Egyptian. She had witnessed enough Egyptians during her line of work.

But what she didn't understand was why this man was watching her with the gaze of a predator. He wanted to masticate her, and his eyes were hungry.

'Where is Prime Minister Tamar?' the emissary asked. 'I was expecting him to be here.'

'You offend me, good sir, for you have such good company with you and you worry about him,' Shukr joked.

'Of course not. I am just wondering if your relationship with the Pharaoh is important to the Prime Minister of this prosperous state.'

For a moment, Shukr was taken aback by the snide comment. 'Of course it is, but I handle the foreign relations while he looks after domestic affairs,' he chuckled, forcing the emissary to laugh too, out of decency. 'Look, Djat Lapis,' he referred to the designation of a minister to the emissary, 'we want to work with the Pharaoh. And I am sure you received a much warmer welcome than any other country right now. We mine the finest gold here which could be traded well in Egypt and we are ready to work that into our relations with you.'

'And in return, you want...spices? That's a strange bargain.'

Not for Gauri. She was well versed in political history and spices was what scented food, and food was what Jambudvipians loved. Armies had to be fed regularly, and so did the people. Spices like coriander and thyme contained in them medicinal properties and they could be woven in as major ingredients in ayurvedic medicines.

'We have our reasons. See, in one way or another, this is just a formality. This trade of ours. One of the most important things we want, Djat Lapis, is to create a relationship with the Pharaoh which is even stronger than it presently is. That if there is an enemy attacking either of our countries, we have each other's backs.'

'But I hear you side with Scythians. They have waged petty battles with us in the past.'

'Who we align with are the ostracised group of Scythians. Not the ones from the North-West frontiers. There is a difference. We would never want to offend a friend by making friends with their enemy.'

The emissary mulled this over. He seemed impressed with all he was getting. Gold was beneficial for Egypt as their currency system had gone for a toss.

'Let me convey this message to the Pharaoh and let's see what he thinks.'

'The question is,' Shukr began with his slimy tone, 'will you put in a good word to him?'

He contemplated. 'Of course, guruji.' He had that foreign accent when he said the native word. 'I always love your hospitality and your...' he trailed off, looking at Gauri, licking his lips, 'people.' She shivered, the apples in her basket moving. His gaze was penetrating and...frightening.

Shukr noticed but gave a plastic smile. 'Sure.'

'I believe we are done then. I shall leave by next week once we discuss further about other matters,' Lapis said, before moving to Gauri and coming close to her.

Shukr was notifying the scribes who were sitting and noting down the discussion between the two, while Lapis caught the opportunity to come closer to Gauri and said: 'What an exquisite creature you are. This skin...it looks bleached,' he said with equal parts awe and disgust.

Gauri didn't speak a word. That was part of the protocol. Not to speak to the guests but remain static. But she felt like screaming.

'Do you suffer from a disease, girl?' Without waiting for her response, he laced his hands around her throat, as if trying to feel the curve of it.

Gauri didn't speak.

'I would love to bed you, girl. A diseased woman will be different for me tonight. I have always been with fit women.'

Gauri didn't move. But she wanted to cry. She could feel her eyes welling up.

And then he came closer still, smelling her, and put his thick, disgusting lips over her fingers, licking them with his serpentine tongue.

I'm going to smash this basket on his head.

She was about to do exactly that when Shukr interrupted, coming partially in between:

'Djat Lapis, two women await your presence in your room.'

'Is that so?' his eyebrows rose in excitement. 'You and your hospitality, guruji,' he chuckled. 'Other countries should learn from you.'

Shukr smiled. Gauri felt a sigh of relief shudder through her.

'But I want her. She seems feisty,' he pointed to Gauri, causing her to go ramrod straight.

Shukr had no excuse anymore. 'Unfortunately, Djat Lapis, she's not a prostitute. She's a servant. We have our roles assigned quite well.'

Lapis wanted to argue and Shukr was impassively watching him, waiting for him to say something that he could override with his kind but snide words. But Lapis conceded.

'As you say, guruji. It is your home I have come to.' As he left, his words seemed innocuous enough, except there was venom in his voice.

Shukr left too.

It was only then that Gauri let out a deep breath. She could feel her heart thumping hard, almost escaping her ribcage. Her knees grew weak and she knelt on the ground, the basket toppling from her hand while she began to wipe the finger he had licked vigorously on the carpet, tears streaming down her face.

She saw Gauri who was now on the floor, laying straight, just taking a deep breath as pain seized her back, for acting as the table for so long. Gauri let out her hand forward, and they both held each other.

For the little time they could.

Djat Lapis had an exhausting day.

He was sweaty, exhausted, and naked, while two fair-skinned women lay on each side of his bed, dozing next to him. He was a lanky but tough man, and the sheets on the mattress were crumpled. The curtains around the bed acted as makeshift protection for him.

He reached for a jug of water, the drink soothing his throat. He liked his job. Going to exotic places. Tasting exotic women.

It was more leisure than work. But he was not happy about how Shukr had handled the situation today. He wanted that weird girl. He wanted to strong-arm her, smack her on the face, and make her his pet on the bed. But Shukr had resisted, and he hadn't wanted to spoil relations with Jambudvipa over a woman.

He closed his eyes and slumbered only to be awakened after a while when he felt something on his body, right under his sheet.

Something was moving.

He arched his brows and lifted the sheet to see his phallus.

And his eyes widened with horror when he saw the spider as big as his hand right next to his most private part.

The arachnid didn't wait. It sank its fangs into the thin skin of the phallus.

And Lapis screamed like no one had ever screamed in years.

When the scream was heard, Gauri was on her way to Mahisha's room. A smile curved up on her face.

She had entered his room when he was sleeping and had put the arachnid close to the sheets. She told the room guards who were stationed outside that she was one of the pleasure women. The Egyptian guards didn't even protest. They allowed her inside. When she came out moments later, she simply told them that the emissary had already fallen asleep and so there was no need for her. They accepted that too. Probably because they were too sleepy themselves.

She reached Mahisha's room. His door was unlike any other. It was golden and had large horns of buffalos, probably the largest she had seen—covering the walls. She touched the tip of it, realising there was dry blood.

Someone had been pierced with it. Probably someone who had harmed Mahisha.

There were two guards here too, but they weren't sheepish in any way. In fact, they were large brutes and looked at her suspiciously.

'Guru Shukr said that I have to clean the room. There's some mess your highness had left behind.'

The guards nodded, allowing her inside, but following her so she wouldn't do any mischief. The security here was too tight.

When she entered the room, she could have noticed the large mattresses, the open windows or the beautiful ceiling, but what assailed her senses was the atrocious smell. A rotten, bloated corpse was floating in the pool.

A frown came upon her face, as Gauri made her way to the pool and began to pull out the woman. She did so singlehandedly while the guard towered over her. The woman now lay flat, discoloured and smelling putrid, from being submerged in the water for quite some time.

She saw that her face had been beaten harshly. Her

mouth was broken, her teeth were missing, likely due to high impact trauma. She was once a beautiful girl who had angered Mahisha.

And this was exactly why Gauri hated him.

He was the epitome of monstrosity. And she was glad that he was about to be killed in the next eight days. The Nine Nights, the operation was called.

She would plunge the blade in him.

Along with Durga.

After all, Gauri worked for her.

5

When she was a child, she had killed a man.

He was coming on to her. He was forcing her against the ground, pinning her roughly. He was kissing her. She was just eight, but the man didn't seem to care. He liked young girls. He liked to touch them and force himself on them. And so, when she kicked him between the legs and he groaned, she grabbed the nearest rock and smacked it right across the man's head.

He lay dead. His skull splintered and broken in two.

For a moment, she was in complete disarray. No tears. No crying. She could feel herself slowly detach from her surroundings and by the time her brother had found her—

She was no more the same person.

Twelve years later, Charini was in a bazaar with Sulochna, her mistress. She worked as a handmaiden, and she carried her jalpa mala everywhere—a string of beads which signified and was the physical manifestation of her belief in Lord Shiva.

And whenever she would brush accidentally against a man in a crowded street, she would feel the touch of that predator from her childhood. Charini would cover herself with enough clothes so her skin would never touch another person. In any way. And she had abstained from violence after her one act on the man. She was never caught, for she was saved from the courts.

But she knew she wouldn't repeat it ever again. The killing. The violence.

And so, when she had agreed to work under Durga, she had only one condition: Don't ask her to kill. That's it.

She became a brahmacharini and devoted herself to Mahadev. But that didn't mean she would not devote herself to Durga's crusade.

'Do you like this?' Her mistress asked to which Charini plainly nodded.

They were in the middle of the busy bazaar amidst hundreds of people. Sulochna liked to come here to see the pearls and necklaces sold by the roadside. She'd rather buy them here than call these shopkeepers to the house.

Charini knew why Sulochna did it. She didn't like being trapped inside her palace all day long. But Charini didn't mind.

She was a petite woman, barely five feet tall, with a round face with deep shadows of dark circles and pale, white lips. She would wear white often as she wanted to keep her colours muted like her face. She remembered how she was as a person long back—all cheery until the incident shook her and made her... emotionally distant from everything.

The bhisak of the village had told her she had accepted the trauma and let it overpower her; thus, she had gone emotionless, but she didn't care. As long as she was surviving, working for a cause, she was fine with it even though she knew that trauma should be acknowledged instead of letting it overpower someone. She knew she had a flaw but she shrugged it off.

'Why am I even asking you? You don't even care. You should...' Sulochna put the pearls next to Charini's ears. 'You should wear it. I'll buy it for you.'

Security was tough. There were five guards moving around Sulochna and Charini.

'No, thank you, my lady,' Charini said, without a smile.

Sulochna groaned and turned to the Captain whose responsibility was to keep Sulochna safe. 'Bashkala, why don't you get the pearls?'

A brute of a man, he had a razor-cut beard over his stretchy skin, and thick, wavy hair that fell to the end of his neck. Bashkala wore dark-coloured armour and from afar he looked scary. But up close, he had the kindest smile Charini had seen.

'My lady, I feel they won't suit me,' he chuckled.

Sulochna growled under her breath. 'Fine. Let's just move on.'

They began to check the other shacks in the bazaar which were in the middle of the street. There were criers who were shouting the latest news, while fruits, spices and vegetables were being sold. There was muslin cloth as well as a few home decoration items up for sale. It was all the more cheap for a woman like Sulochna.

She was a beautiful woman. When Charini had first seen her, she was in awe of her beauty. She had round eyes and a way of wearing kohl that was slanted in a unique fashion. She had cherry-coloured lips and straight, onyx hair flowing till her ankles that she would braid perfectly. It was safe to say that Charini was jealous of her mistress' beauty.

'The pearls would have suited you,' Bashkala whispered to Charini when Sulochna was busy scouring around the shops.

'I don't care,' Charini said flatly.

'Why are you so strange? You sound...'

She looked at him sharply. But there was still no emotion. 'If you think I'm strange, you don't have to talk to me.'

'See, even the way you said that, it had no...anger.'

'You want me to be angry?'

'I want you to display some kind of emotion. It'll be good for a sunny day like this.'

As Sulochna was nearing the end of the market, Charini saw a brawl had taken place between two strangers. As the mistress was close to it, Charini grabbed her hand and pulled her away while Bashkala shouted and tried to diffuse the situation. But the men didn't stop. They began to push Bashkala, so his other guards came to take control, and they began to beat the man.

There was a lot of commotion. Lots of people began to push and prod each other. Charini felt lost in the maze of people and she was almost confused for a moment, her bleary vision going back to the time when her brother was killed by Mahisha's men for stealing from their camp.

He had gone there to steal for Charini, as they were orphans and poor.

Charini was waiting for him in the forest with a hungry stomach.

But the wait lasted twelve years.

He never returned from the camp, and later she

learned that he was impaled and displayed to show that thievery was not accepted in Mahisha's new empire, especially from his honourable countrymen.

She blinked and she was shaken up to realise Bashkala was standing in front of her.

'Where is Lady Sulochna?'

'What?'

'Where is she?' he rasped.

'I was holding her...' she looked at the hand and found it empty.

Sulochna had vanished.

Charini was sitting on the ground of her room, after leaving the commotion of the market as Bashkala's men were questioning and throwing anyone they suspected in prison. They emptied the entire bazaar to find Sulochna, but it all seemed in vain.

Charini had her arms around herself in an embrace when Bashkala came in, his face white.

'She's gone. How could you let her out of your sight?' he said gruffly.

'She's not a child, captain. I was holding her hand, nonetheless. I thought she was with me and I didn't see any suspicious person around,' she scolded him.

He flared his nostrils.

'What do you think it is?'

'Kidnapping, of course. The brawl was fake. When we apprehended the two fighters, they admitted that they were paid by a hooded stranger to perform the brawl so a commotion could be created. We are going to interrogate them for more information, but I don't think they know much,' Bashkala informed her before groaning in frustration.

Charini raised her brows. Person? She was glad they didn't say it was a *woman*.

She had disguised herself quite well when she had approached these men. They were actors from a travelling troupe. And they would face the brunt for being part of the kidnapping they didn't even know would happen. But Charini didn't care, as long as the work was done.

It was the first of the Nine Nights. On her end, the first part of the mission was complete.

Sulochna—wife of the Prime Minister Tamar of Mahishapur—had officially been kidnapped.

6

70 miles from the Carwar Port, modern day Karnataka...

The mission was simple.

Working for Durga meant going undercover for three to five years. Each participant would work their way into the social hierarchy of Mahisha's empire. Hidden in plain sight. They would enter like a ghost and behave as if they followed their supreme king. Charini was supposed to get close to Tamar and Gauri was supposed to get close to Shukr. And when the Nine Nights clock would begin, their real job of taking down pawns would also begin. Because their goal was to eliminate Mahisha from the map of Jambudvipa.

And while the rest of the crew were quite the serious and determined kind, Chandra was the only one who would take the mission in a playful stride, as her job required her to do. But then, she was a playful person since birth. She was the only one who didn't have any personal reason to join Durga's crusade. She did it solely because she wanted to be part of a revolution. And Durga was. Plus, being in risky and dangerous situations was always nice.

So, when she was told to get close to the Navatakavechas—a bunch of ocean raiders—she gladly accepted her task and worked her way up the ranks to become a boatswain.

The Navatakavechas were a bunch of legal buccaneers,

sanctioned by Mahisha to carry out illegal looting and plundering of sanctioned foreign ships or native rebel ships that sailed on the Sindhu Sagar. They had the best of weaponry as well as the deadliest of soldiers on it. They would regularly risk their lives, and their life expectancy was not more than thirty years. And though they would do it for Mahisha, they would keep a portion of the loot before giving it to their king. Mahisha knew of this practice, but he didn't mind for they did their job well.

So, Chandra was glad that she was able to survive for three years straight—first she was ridiculed for being a woman on the ship, then showing her skills and impressing the Admiral, and then finally demonstrating how good she was at organising food and water storage. She had earned her position over a period of time and had to tirelessly work for it.

When Chandra's day had begun, the first day of the Nine Nights, she saw the letter again which she had kept safely under her bed. It was given to her by a young messenger back at the Carwar fish market, and it read:

The Nine Nights have begun.
Ship sails from Ceylon on the 5th day.

That was it, along with a bunch of coordinates for her to navigate when she would set sail.

Four days more to reach the stretch between Ceylon and Jambudvipa.

Race against time? She hated this.

Ugh.

The boatswain's job was right under the quartermaster in the hierarchy. And it was to make sure the food was fresh. Taste it. Make changes to it. Keep checking storage barrels as well as loot barrels. Having an idea of how much of the spiced wine called maireya was being drunk. And they would drink a lot.

She had to also look at the cargo and check if anything else was missing or not. The deck had to be cleaned. The captain's cabin too. And all the other little nitty-gritties. The Navatakavechas quartermaster was a pain in the ass.

His name was Utharaka and he had the nose of a hawk. Pointy with large, gaping holes for nostrils. She would make jokes about his fat nostrils but on the face, she would smile at him. He had white hair on the side of his large ears and a bald, freckled head. He had tired eyes, underlined by severe eye bags which made him look ancient. He came in front of her when she was in the kitchen directing the women.

'When do you plan to start looking like a girl?' the quartermaster blurted.

'When you stop treating women like shit,' she grinned.

He sighed. 'There's a spillover in the cargo room. Get it cleaned, woman.'

'As you say, my good sir,' she bowed, but cursed at him under her breath.

Chandra had her hair cut short like a boy's. Small with streaks of purple. She had a lanky body and wore a dhoti which was a boy's garment, worn to cover the lower part of the body but she didn't care. Clothing can't define someone's gender and she knew that. A tight cloth was wrapped around her upper chest, and a shawl was draped diagonally over that. But the most striking was the symbol of a moon, shaped like a sickle in the middle of her forehead, which she had gotten from her grandmother when she was eight years old. Inked with needles. It was a painful and a bloody process, but she knew the symbol meant that life and death were part of a seasonal cycle. And she liked that idea, since she had got it made just after she'd lost her mother.

Ignoring her thoughts from the past, she did what she was told, moving for the cargo room, when from the main deck she heard—

'Attention everyone!'

Chandra and Utharaka exchanged a glance before they made their way upstairs to face the Admiral.

He was in a navy blue dhoti, and he had a chiselled, scarred body with jet black hair and a thin, twirled up moustache. The only thing that made him look more than an ordinary sailor was his plated jewellery that had a serpent's eye. There were three dozen men amongst whom Chandra stood and the other men were rowing the oars.

'We are at another parade of triumph,' the Admiral began, standing up on the ledge of the ship, holding the many strings that were connected to the sails. 'Look at the east and understand what you see.'

All did look at what he was pointing at. Chandra saw a vessel. It was a trireme. One sail. Multiple masts. A thick, broad hull, and a hundred oars. It was a Greek ship with approximately a hundred and fifty sailors on it. It could be returning from a naval battle or perhaps delivering cargo. The reason was not important. What was important was...

'We have to take it down. Greeks have never been King Mahisha's greatest ally. Why don't we just have some fun? They could be carrying pork, olive oil or pottery.'

'But it's a trireme, ours is a plava,' one of the sailors said with a dead spirit, referring to the type of ship that the Jambudvipians had—it could withstand storms but held lesser people than the trireme. 'It will be difficult.'

The Admiral looked at the man who had spoken up. 'Your attitude is what makes you, my dear friend. Never believe the enemy is strong. Fight. Fight and fight till you succeed,' he made a fist in the air.

He was a charming man. And Chandra couldn't help but grin whenever she looked at him. When the Admiral saw her flashing her teeth at him, he smiled back at her. He liked her, she knew. He would flirt with her and tell her how gorgeous her violet hair looked. And she would nod, bow, and go away. Perhaps, giggle sometimes.

'What do you say, girl?' he asked in front of the hundred soldiers. 'What should be our plan?'

All eyes were on her.

She could have gone nervous, but she put her hands on either side of her waist and said: 'Offensive. Attack them without giving them time to counter.'

'Hee-yah!' the Admiral grinned. 'That's the spirit! Chandra, I want you to join the boarding this time.'

She widened her eyes, 'Really?'

'Of course, my dear girl.'

Utharaka interfered, snapping in between. 'She's a woman, Admiral.'

Didn't you just moments ago say I didn't look like a girl? Chandra thought.

'The seas don't care whether you're a man or woman. The seas only care if the spirit is high or nigh,' he grinned and hooted loudly. His men did so as well. 'Prepare your grappling hooks, move the vessel towards them, gather the archers and aim and load the catapults, my dear friends. WE ARE GOING TO BATTLE!'

And for a moment, Chandra was glad to be with someone like the Admiral.

The attack was swift.

It was the plava that was making way towards the Greek ship. For a moment, the foreigners were confused. They had their spyglasses close to their eyes. Watching. And as they began to announce their defence—the arrows had begun flying.

The Admiral shouted orders. The archers flung oil dipped arrows high in the air, blanketing the stormy clouds till they fell like rains of carnage, pounding and piercing the Greek soldiers. It plunged into their sockets or their skulls or their legs, unable to move. It was a rainfall of chaos.

Catapults with fire balls were shot. Chandra could see the men loading them up with precision. They smacked and created dents close to the foremast, the main mast, as well as the bowsprit.

The sky had opened up by now—it was pouring. Thunder raged on.

'DO NOT BE FRIGHTENED BY THE GODS OF THE WATER, MY FRIENDS! ATTACK! ATTACK!' the Admiral shouted with gusto. 'QUARTERMASTER! WHEEL IT CLOSE FOR THE BOARDING!'

Utharaka from the quarter deck nodded and instantly beat the drums that guided the oarsmen to move the ship closer to the Greek vessel.

Chandra had a dhanush and arrows in her hands. And on her back she carried a bronze shield.

The Admiral came by then, close to her and said: 'Are you ready, girl?'

His men had begun to get the planks they would require for boarding.

And then the raging fires of chaos came showering over their deck. It was the first wave of attack and quickly, Chandra pulled out the shield and guarded both her and the Admiral. The impact of the arrows shook her up, but she knelt down and held her ground till it stopped. When she saw her shield, the arrows, she realised, had dented the bronze. She got rid of the arrows with the help of the bow and turned to the startled Admiral: 'What do you think?'

He grinned. He had a symbols inked over his entire body.

'Let's do it then.'

The two vessels crashed into each other, splintering with the impact. The planks were kept on the other ship and Chandra stormed forward, leaving along with the rest of the soldiers. She spat the rainwater as she shot the arrows, one by one.

One hit an enemy's head, while another the chest. It was a flurry. A daze. Everything was moving rapidly, flashing by. There were blood and guts spilled all over the place. She kept slipping because of the watery board, but she didn't care. She got up and fought valiantly; even when someone came close with a blade, she deflected it with her bow, pulled out an arrow and stabbed the man with it, piercing the blade deep into his eye socket and pulled it out.

As she aimed her arrow at the archer who was standing in the crow's nest and was shooting from there—

She was pushed and tossed on the ground. She fell next to a headless corpse. Coming to her feet, she searched around to see who had thrown her back. It was a fair-skinned, green-eyed soldier of the Greeks. A brute, twice her size who had a blade in his hand. As he came forward, storming towards her, she pulled out her shield from the back and shoved it against his face. It met his forehead with a thud and the impact confused him. Then she slammed the edge of the shield against his chest and pulled him down.

She punched him hard, until his teeth were all knocked out.

'Great going, girl!' she heard the Admiral. But in all the blurriness and the dangerous daze of excitement, fire, and fury rising on the enemy deck, she couldn't see him. Her eyes were trying to catch hold of him, until she found him on the wooden rods that led to the mast. He was locked in a dangerous sword fight with the captain of the Greek ship, by the looks of it.

The Admiral was majestic, swift in his sword weilding, but then she noticed the ship was keeling.

She pulled an arrow and shot at the captain. Aiming right at the head. He dropped dead.

'What did you do that for?' he cried out, disappointed.

'The ship is drowning. We need to get the cargo. That's more important.'

He raised his brows and proudly grinned. 'Great job, girl!'

The ship was manoeuvring from left to right and to right to left. It was moving haphazardly and water sloshed against its sides, filling the corridors of the vessel below the deck. Huge, gaping holes had been created from where ocean water was entering.

Any moment now, they would go down with the ship and it would be a big mess.

The Admiral and Chandra reached the lowest level of the cargos, where they saw two guards who were planning to run.

Chandra didn't have time to waste. She brought two arrows to her bowstring and shot them simultaneously. The arrows sliced through thin air and pierced the foreheads of the guards, who fell down.

'That's some military handiwork!' the Admiral exclaimed as they broke through the doors of the cargo to see the large jars and glass bottles of olive oil.

The ship veered precariously to the left and they both fell to one side of the wall, when Chandra saw a huge barrel rolling towards them. If it hit them, they would be knocked unconscious.

With a quick shift of her body, she pulled up her legs and broke through the incoming barrel.

The ship came back to its normal position and the Admiral went for the most important cargo—barrels that held sugar, salt and olive oil. Five barrels. That was it. Not much else was needed.

They began to roll it up to the main deck.

By the time the barrels were loaded on their ship and most enemies were dead on theirs, Chandra realised the ship had begun to sink. It was going down.

Her heart began to scream for help, as the Admiral jumped over his ship and he told her to jump too.

She was the last one behind.

She began to move onto the plank as the ship began to sink deep into the water, when someone caught her leg and she fell on the watery board.

She saw it was a half-moving, legless man who was holding on to her, so she would die with them.

She kicked him in the face, till the point that his skull broke and his eyes went blank. Then she scurried forward, moving for the ledge...

'MOVE FAST!' the Admiral's voice boomed.

And she did. With a clenched jaw, she lurched.

She was suspended in air for a moment when she made that jump, reaching for the ledge of her ship, when she realised, she was not going to come close to the ledge and would probably drown...

Her hand was grabbed!

She felt her legs move aimlessly as she was held onto firmly by none other than the Admiral. He was holding her, with a charming smile and a tough face. And he pulled her up.

As she came on board, he hugged her tightly.

The men were surprised that she was able to survive this on-board action, and some even clapped quietly while Utharaka peered from the corner, with a hawk-like gaze.

'Good job, dear old friend!' he patted her on the back and then cupped her face. 'Good job, indeed. I'm proud of you,' he whispered.

Chandra smiled weakly. She was happy. Real happy. But also sad as they all were cheering and hurraying the Admiral. She was told that because the Nine Nights had begun, so had her real work.

'Today we shall get drunk and retch in the seas!' he declared as if it were something grand.

She liked it here. A lot. She saw the Admiral again, who was moving for his cabin. He winked at her before he went out of her sight.

She liked him too.

But she had a mission.

And in that mission, the first part of her job was to gain the Admiral's trust.

Second, which was the hardest:

To *kill* him.

7

Mahisha rode on his stallion towards the inside of Kanchipuram.

His heart thumped with each jerk the animal made. Behind him, hundreds of men followed. His commander, Trinetra, followed him too, but at his own pace. Mahisha could easily sit in a driven chariot and while his time away sleeping or eating like other kings before him.

But no. Not him.

He was always in action. His muscles were protruded and his face was impassive. He wore a huge, thick crown with two iron buffalo horns.

He had always liked the majestic animal and when he had learnt that buffaloes represented aggression and strength, he made it his totem, his way of looking at life too. He now considered himself as part of the buffalo.

Kanchipuram was mostly forests, woods, and dried clearings with the Vegavathi river flowing to its southwest. There were hills on the horizon and temples all around. Mahisha had had them built them with sculptures of his face as well as those of his generals.

As he stepped onto the clayey ground, he noticed the Panas who had camped themselves there. Mahisha had allowed them to come here and be his guest. He had asked them to enter Mahishapur, but they had politely rejected saying that they would only step into the city as their allies and not just as potential allies.

But they agreed to come close to Maisuru, as a gesture of goodwill.

Their envoys were usually rude and offensive when delivering their messages, but Mahisha had a habit of putting his ego aside and listening to other people.

Being a king didn't just mean to be ruthless. It meant being diplomatic as well. His daunting personality and tall stature could often fool a person into thinking he was just brawn, but he was as much a myth as him being an asura with the head of a buffalo. The Aryas were only good at spreading propaganda, lies, and defamatory statements.

He could see that the Panas were in abundance. Close to a couple of hundreds, all spread widely, with bonfires lit and cooking pork for themselves. There were many with their families wearing fur and teal-coloured armour, helmets with of the shape of a bird sculpted on top of it.

And then there were a few who had skull-shaped symbols on their helmets and those were the tough, strong fighters.

For the longest time, Panas were nomadic. They didn't belong anywhere. But when he learnt that they had crossed the borders of Dasas and entered the Southern territory—he was ecstatic, even though they had killed his men. He had sent his envoy to inform them that he would like to partner with them.

And they accepted, which was a surprise. He wanted their expertise in warfare and could use them as paid mercenaries to weed out the rebels, without losing any of his close men in the midst of the ordeal.

It was safe to say, however, that he was disappointed. The Panas rode in thousands, and here, only hundreds resided.

He was stopped at the entrance of the camp.

'Yes?' the soldier spoke.

'Tell them King Mahisha is here,' he announced.

The soldiers nervously looked at each other and allowed him in. He rode inside atop his stallion, along with his men. There were lanes and cramped up places. There were bear traps kept on the outskirts as well as fences dug up, to make sure no one would enter from outside. They had made this little place, given by Mahisha, their home.

When he came to the clearing, he dismounted, realising all the Panas had come out. The children were shoved back, away from him.

Mahisha watched everyone in awe, as he pulled off his crown and handed it to Trinetra, who had dismounted behind him.

He noticed how the Panas were wearing mute colours and they had rich, textured fair skin, with glimmering irises of the colour grey. The men wore capes of fur and carried daggers alongside their boots and pants. They had thick girdles with empty sheaths while women were in rags and loins.

'Welcome, Mahisha,' he heard the voice.

Mahisha swivelled his head to find a tall man entering. Though the man had a skull helmet, covering most of his face, he was holding a battle axe and his physique was hidden behind tufts of fur and sheaths of pigskin.

'Chief Thamisada?' Mahisha asked to confirm. Thamisada was the one he was in contact with through messages. He was the *arpada,* the leader of the Panas.

He nodded.

Mahisha smiled as he came forward and pressed the man's hand tightly. 'I believe you are comfortable here.'

'More so than you can imagine. We have begun to form a liking for Kanchi,' he said in a gruff, low tone as if he had a sore throat.

Alongside him, a man entered but he was wearing a woman's gown and had kohl around his eyes. For a moment, Mahisha was figuring out which gender he belonged to, and when the man spoke, he spoke like a woman but had the voice of a man.

'I'm the *enaree* of the camp, your highness,' he bowed. 'My name is Rigoli.'

'Enaree?' Mahisha raised his brows.

'A soothsayer, a priest.'

'You predict the future?'

He smiled. 'Yes, I do.'

Mahisha wanted to chuckle but the Panas had their customs and their own ranks—so he respected that. 'I am quite disappointed though. I was expecting more from you.'

'There are more. They are stationed four flanks of Kanchi, hidden in plain sight.' Thamisada replied. 'If anything happens to us..." he began in an ominous note, 'they will know and they will come.'

For a moment, Mahisha was taken aback. *This man is prepared.* He should have been offended at being threatened, but he was glad he was going to make an alliance with a strong breed of warriors and their leader.

'Shall we begin then?'

Thamisada looked at Rigoli and chuckled. All the other Panas watched the conversation quietly, but they smirked at what Mahisha had just said.

And then Thamisada came close to Mahisha and said, 'We have a different way of inaugurating guests, my friend. We do not just begin with business. We first create relations.'

Mahisha shrugged. 'Okay. How?'

Holding a fat, disgusting, muddy swine and making it hover over a pot of boiling water was not what he had in mind for the initiation. There was a drink that was passed around, and there was fire that crackled in between. The smell of the woods, and the swine, and the drinks was intoxicating, and the sound of the Panas dancing and beating their drums came from afar.

But it was evening, and apparently this animal sacrifice was important to build relations with Panas.

The lengths people went to in order to appease others boggled his mind, but he dropped the swine in the water, heard its grunts. Everyone began to clap while Rigoli chanted:

"*Erdimpas, bless this union! BLESS THIS UNION!*" he screamed at the top of his voice.

Mahisha waited for something more to happen. Perhaps more animals would be sacrificed or... something. Anything.

But nothing.

The pig was dead and was ordered to be gutted and displayed on the outskirts to make sure Erdimpas, the virgin goddess according to Rigoli, would not let anyone enter with disregard and trouble the alliance in any way.

Thamisada came in the middle, hugged Mahisha and announced, 'TONIGHT, WE SHALL FEAST!'

'Do they even want an alliance?' Trinetra asked Mahisha, as they ate the roasted leg of a chicken.

'Everyone has a custom, commander. We must be patient.'

There were other important soldiers sitting in a circle in the largest tent of the camp, and Thamisada was seated right next to Mahisha and Trinetra, though he was laughing and joking with his peers. His helmet was still on.

'You know with the scare of Durga around us, we should travel back fast,' Trinetra said. 'Not waste time here.'

'You speak like Shukr. I brought you here and not Shukr because you don't behave like him,' Mahisha scoffed.

They all had jars of white milk in their hands, which they had been served. Mahisha looked at the milky concoction; it looked familiar. 'What is in this, chief?' he asked Thamisada.

'Somas,' he responded.

Mahisha blinked. He wanted to throw it away. He could hear Trinetra almost gasp in horror that a Dasa was given an Arya's drink. However, Mahisha just smiled. 'But why?'

'When we had entered the country,' Thamisada began, 'our people were the first ones to find the Somalata plant. We squeezed it, mixed it with goat milk and drank it. We went into another world, Mahisha. We saw ourselves. We became the better version of us. Our minds opened and we became better warriors. The Aryas caught on to our culture and practice after imitating us. Pooh!' he spat on the ground. 'Thieves!'

Mahisha didn't know it was the Scythians who brought the drink to Jambudvipa. He always associated it as the drinks of the Aryas.

'But this…' he pointed loudly so Thamisada's peers could also hear, 'is why the Aryas fell in these lands. They indulged in it too much.' It had made it easier for him to take over, as they were drunk on it and were not able to strategise clearly.

'Because they are weak!' And when he said it, his peers laughed.

Fire burnt in the corner and the women were waving fans at them.

'Are you weak, Mahisha?' Thamisada asked. 'If you are, you can keep it down. We will not force our guest to drink something he doesn't want to.'

Mahisha looked at the milk again. He had never tasted the Somas and he had never wanted to. He knew it could potentially destroy the soul. But he also knew that in front of the Pana chief—who represented strength—he had to be strong. He had to show he was like them. Worthy of having an alliance with.

'Don't do it, your highness,' Trinetra's voice came as a whisper.

But he didn't listen.

'Aren't you doing it?' he asked Thamisada.

The chief was definitely grinning.

'Oh, I am.'

He lifted a bit of his skull helmet to bring the bowl close to his lips.

Mahisha did so as well.

And they both swallowed it, even the peers. After Mahisha finished, he handed Trinetra a drink too. He could feel the sourness of the milk latching on to his tongue and making him feel a bit weird and wobbly in the head.

But he didn't feel anything else after that.

'So...how am I supposed to feel?' he asked.

'It will come to you.'

'What will I see?'

With a brief shake of his head, Thamisada said, 'Yourself.'

By the time he went to bed, Mahisha was feeling weird.

Everything was moving in a drastic and spectacularly bizarre fashion where he was not able to concentrate on anything. Sounds of bells began echoing in his ears. He could hear the gushing water of the river.

He fell on his mattress even though Thamisada had

left him a beautiful Pana virgin on his bed. He didn't seem to care. He was too busy staring into nothingness with his wide, dilated pupils. He was watching the simple ground on which he lay while he felt the girl's hands lap around his back.

'Are you okay, master?' she asked.

Her voice came as a faint whisper and he turned to see her face. She resembled someone.

Someone from his past.

And then he saw.

It was his mother. Rambha.

Her eyes brown...her square jaw, and her white hair.

'Are you okay, darling?'

'Maa...' he sighed. 'You are alive.'

'I am always alive, darling.'

'How...how...'

Her hands went over his hair and she patted them. 'You'll be fine.'

'How am I...' he was shivering, sweating. 'But but...I saw you die.'

'No, my dear. I am here with you. Do you love your mother?'

His eyes moistened, 'I do.' And then he began to cry.

She hugged him tightly and he wrapped his arms around her.

'Why did you have to leave me? Why did you...'

'It was your father.'

'I know.'

He knew very well indeed. He would see his father beat his mother every day. He'd be drunk on madira and smack her with a girdle of some kind. He was a local buffalo farmer of the Toda clan. And she...she was an ostracised Arya woman. She was pushed out for she didn't believe in their customs. She sought happiness in a farmer, but he treated her like livestock.

Since his childhood, Mahisha had witnessed the unbridled torture his father had meted out to his mother. So much so, that he had normalised it. He began to believe that that was how women were to be treated. They had to be slapped around. They had to be shoved in the corner. They were objects.

'She's my slave.'

His father had said to him, when Mahisha had tried to intervene once.

'You should have spoken back to him. You should have slapped him back,' he spoke now through soft sobs.

'I was not strong enough,' Rambha looked melancholic. 'I still regret not fighting back.'

'Why? Because you were bruised all the time?'

'No, my dear. But because if I had, you wouldn't have turned into the monster you are today,' she said, and her eyes turned red as she grabbed hold of him tightly by the throat and began to choke him. He wanted to pull out, but he was too tightly held.

'No...no...' he coughed.

'The only noble thing you ever did, child, was kill your father. After that, you became a reflection of him!' she rasped, and he could feel he was counting his last breath.

Then the grasp was gone and his vision returned. He once again found himself in the tent with the virgin, who was trying to pat him hurriedly.

'Are you okay, your highness?' she asked.

But he couldn't speak. His tongue and mouth felt dry. Everything was numb.

And he closed his eyes.

The morning had dawned, and Mahisha, when he woke up, could see no woman next to him. He sighed. The effects were dying off and he already felt better than he was earlier. He didn't like the hallucination he had had. It brought unsavoury memories that stressed him out.

Staggering, he moved out of the tent, rubbing his eyes when he saw Trinetra walking towards him.

'There's some problem,' he said, cutting right to the chase. 'You look like...was it the Soma? I know. I had pretty bad nightmares.'

Well, nightmare was an understatement as to what Mahisha had felt and seen. He was always proud of killing a lot of people, but he wasn't proud of letting his mother die. And he never revealed that his inability to protect her had led to an innocent person getting killed.

'It's just a bright fucking morning, Trinetra.' He was slouching and he wanted to wash his face and wipe his dry mouth. 'What could have happened?'

He didn't speak for a moment, trying to cough up words that would make the most sense. 'I think you should listen to the madman yourself.'

Mahisha, with this disoriented limp, entered the big tent where Thamisada and Rigoli were sitting with their knees on the ground. They had a lot of papers in the front of them, scattered. When Mahisha saw it, he saw what was drawn over it. It had a woman with ten arms on a tiger and she held various weapons in her hand.

'You have some explaining to do, Mahisha,' Thamisada said in a stern tone.

'What happened?' Mahisha asked in a defeated voice.

'Rigoli saw something yesterday.'

'Like a prophecy?' Mahisha gurgled a chuckle. Magic was the last thing he believed in.

But Thamisada didn't find humour in it. 'She saw your enemy.'

'I have many. You have to be specific,' he mundanely suggested.

The chief signalled at the woman.

'Durga.'

Mahisha picked up the piece of paper. 'How does she have ten hands?'

'It's not funny, Mahisha. Who is she?'

'Some assassin,' he said nonchalantly. 'My men are taking care of her in Mahishapur. She's apparently hidden as a spy inside the city and we will weed her out. She's no problem.'

'No point,' Rigoli whispered and Mahisha saw that she was pale as a ghost right now.

'What do you mean?' he asked, a slight crease between his brows.

Rigoli's eyes shot up. 'Because she's *not* in Mahishapur. She's *here* amongst us, one of us!'

8

The second day of the Nine Nights had begun.

She was tending to her tiger, Dawon, when he growled softly. Seksh, if he got the message, would be here by the next evening and she had to be well prepared.

'How do you feel, boy?' she asked. She had wrapped him up in cloth strips and had put balm on his wounds made up of several medicinal leaves.

The tiger moaned.

'Still hurts?'

Dawon came on his feet. Or at least, he struggled on his four paws, as she hugged him tightly and patted him on the head.

'You'll be fine.'

He tried to walk for a while, but she could see he was putting too much pressure on his legs to stay stable.

I shouldn't take his assistance for a while now. He'll get worse if he fights.

'Your dependence on that creature will result in our operation's failure,' a voice beckoned.

The outpost was supposed to be empty, so she pulled out her dagger, scanning the place. Her jaw tightened, as rays of sunlight split into yellow threads. And then she saw the man.

He was right there. Standing with a long sitar in his hand, a mule by his side, matted hair with a flower garland around it. He had a perpetual smile on his face, but that didn't mean he was happy. It could be sinister too.

She knew who it was.

The messenger of the Aryas.

Narad.

If General Seksh ever had nightmares, it would be of the young boy he had killed in his hut. He was a helpless kid. Barely eighteen, perhaps, trying to protect the woman he loved. And Seksh was callous enough to bring his blade inside of him and let him succumb to his death. And then he went for the woman. The young girl Mahisha had desired to woo and pleasure, but she had run away to the forest by then.

Later, Mahisha had gotten angry at Seksh for not able to deliver. But he got himself busy with the multitudes of other women he had in his harem.

Seksh was lying down naked, a crimson sheet wrapped around his private parts, while he aimlessly replayed that day in his head. He had killed a lot of people to appease Mahisha, but that one kill he regretted. If he had a way to move back in time, he wouldn't have killed that man.

'What are you thinking about?' Asiloma asked, who lay next to him, cuddling him and kissing him on the neck.

Seksh smiled at his lover. For some reason, he never understood Mahisha's indulgence in women. Seksh was different. He had begun feeling different when he was young. He was fascinated by the frames and curves of men more than women. And it made him feel like an outcast. That was until he met Asiloma. They found love in the oddest of places—in the most regressive empire of Jambudvipa, led by Mahisha. Seksh had not told his childhood friend and ruler about his lover. If Mahisha knew it was another man, he would be expelled from the post and imprisoned. Or worse, killed.

Mahisha had a lot of good qualities. But tolerance was not one of them. So, to appease him, Seksh would act more like a loyalist than a mere follower. He would be his dog and appease his thoughts even if he didn't agree with them.

'About how we were handpicked by Shukr to learn the ways of starting a revolution.'

Asiloma smiled. 'Why was that old man even interested in bringing a change like this? Did he lose someone to the Aryas?'

'No. We don't know much as well. He called himself an agent of revolution and we were his weapons. But more than that, when I dug deep into his past, I realised his daughter had escaped and run away to the Aryas when she was quite young. Few days later, while frantically searching for her, he was told that she had died under mysterious circumstances. He was certain that she had died.'

'Why did she run away?'

'Probably because he was a compulsive, controlling man,' Seksh sighed. He knew how Shukr could be. Absolutely, infuriatingly irritating.

'Wow. That's tragic.'

Sheksh turned to his newly appointed lieutenant. 'We have to leave.' His jaw was clenched.

His face moved from a smile to a frown. 'I know.'

It was their last night together for the foreseeable future.

For he had received a message from the dreadful Durga. She had managed to take down an entire outpost and she was waiting for him.

'What does she want? Why would she reveal herself like this?' Asiloma asked.

'I think she's being overconfident or she's not Durga,' he replied with certainty. His experience in military had taught him to always peel the layers of the situation one was given.

He began to dress up, wear his long uttaran and a tunic. 'It could be an ambush. And I can't risk that.'

Asiloma was still in bed, propped up on one hand. 'Look at you. You are a smart man.'

'I don't underestimate my enemies because they are from the opposite gender. The rebels, no matter how few, have continued to exist till now. Their survival is because they are smart. And we need to take down this Durga with smartness,' he paused to look at Asiloma and smiled. 'I love you. But I'll go first. You leave a few hours later. Sleep, if you want.'

'I know the drill, general,' he mockingly added his title. 'The drill of lying to everyone.'

Seksh had already ordered his men to carry chariots of armoury and he was bringing more than a hundred people to the outpost.

He was ready.

'Dawon is useful,' she told Narad.

'No. He's a liability,' his tone was cold and terrible.

She hated him. Probably because he was a very calculative, shrewd, and rude man but would always have a smile lingering on his face that would disarm anyone. He was close to being middle-aged, with flecks of grey in his sideburns.

'You want me to get rid of him?' she asked with a sigh at the end.

'Do you understand the gravity of this mission, girl?' Narad snapped.

'I do. We have been preparing for this for the longest time.'

'Exactly,' he said sharply.

'Why are you here?'

'To see whether you are ready or not.'

'I am.'

'Have the bodies been disposed of?'

'Yes, sir. Burnt.'

'You do realise he'll be here shortly? Seksh cannot be underestimated.'

'I don't plan to underestimate him.'

'He's a smart man.'

'I know.'

'But emotional,' he said it as if having emotions was a weapon that could backfire at someone. 'Use it.'

She didn't like all this handholding. And she knew Narad wouldn't go to any of the other girls and speak to them like this. He trusted them. But not her. She had come late to the gathering. Quite late. But she had proved her worth.

'Good. Very good. Get rid of the animal then,' he turned to leave.

She couldn't see his face properly as he mounted on his mule and with a slight whistle, moved for the gate and left, as if he was never here.

She looked at Dawon, who was still limping, and she patted him on the face, then snapped her fingers twice. The tiger looked astonished for a moment and then with a brief nod, he left the outpost.

He was sad that he couldn't contribute to the mission.

And she was sad that she couldn't even hug him goodbye.

Seksh looked at his cook for a moment. There were two things he infinitely loved. One was the arms of his lover and the other was the food that he was given. The cook was a woman. A hairless one at that. She looked like a sick child, with her lanky, sunken cheekbones.

But she cooked marvelously. The smell of herbs and roasted goat was just enough to set his spirits soaring up. And that was the kind of food he wanted before leaving to defeat Durga.

'Why don't you come with me?' he asked the cook jovially.

'But my lord...um...' the cook was shivering. Her fingers were laced together and she looked worried.

'What is the problem?'

'I have a family here.'

For a moment, Seksh couldn't believe her words.

He was infuriated. 'Do you think I care? I am going for a fight and I get hungry. So you come along with me. It's not a bloody request. It's an order.'

The cook, for a moment, was taken aback and nodded glumly.

'Great,' he smiled. Sometimes, asserting power was important. He happily dug into the feast in front of him. And as he was about to take his first bite, he heard the voice:

'You are one brainy little shit, aren't you? Pompous like your stupid king.'

Seksh was almost taken aback as to who had the guts to speak to him like that. But it was a cranky old man's voice which had burst in through the main doors, with no guard interfering with his presence.

Shukr.

Seksh growled under his breath, realising he shouldn't have sent a messenger about Durga to him.

Here goes my apetite.

'What happened, guruji?'

'No, please. Have two gallons of wine too before you leave,' Shukr scowled mockingly. 'That assassin has literally displayed herself in the open and you are here. Feasting.' There was an extra bite to his last word.

'It's a full day's journey. And it's an ambush. My men are preparing weapons and sharpening them while chariots are being loaded. It takes time, guruji,' Seksh shrugged.

'I don't care if it's an ambush. If there's a chance it's the assassin, I want you to bring her back. Alive. We could use some intelligence regarding the rebels.'

'And what makes you think she will respond?'

'We shall torture her to death,' Shukr leaned on the table. But Seksh just chuckled to himself.

'Was I being funny?'

'I don't think it's Durga.'

'What do you mean?'

'Don't you think it's strange that the moment you learn about her, she announces her entry? This is some bloody gutsy person in the empire who knew about the information your spy gave and is being funny with us.'

Shukr, for a moment, contemplated with this idea. 'You could be right. It could be someone harmless. Or an ambush. Or a decoy. Or it could really be Durga, since she happened to wipe out the entire outpost by herself.'

'She had a tiger,' he whispered.

'What?'

'She had a tiger with her,' he said, louder this time.

'So, a woman and a tiger wipe out an outpost and you believe she's just doing it to be funny?'

Seksh realised he was wrong in assuming that and he almost bit his tongue.

'What I mean to say is, you can be right or wrong, but you'll only know it if you bloody go there rather than spend your time on this stupid feast.'

Seksh came up on his feet, pushing his chair away. 'All right, I'm going.'

'We cannot take a chance. Durmukha is coming with a lot of gold and silver—so much that our treasury will be flowing in abundance for the next hundred years. We need that money because we are already going in debt, thanks to Mahisha's relentless, useless campaigns against the rebels. We cannot take even a tiny risk.' He was talking about the minister of finance, the treasury head.

Seksh nodded. He didn't eat the food.

But he glanced at the cook to direct her to pack her things. He swivelled his head to the other direction of the room where Asiloma had come through another door, decked in his armour, looking at Seksh with worry about being scolded like a child.

I'm coming for you, Durga.

9

Her mission was a little more complicated than the rest of the girls'. And since the Nine Nights had begun, she had to start thinking of ideas.

Gauri didn't have a particular object to find, or lure someone, or kidnap someone, or do anything like that. She had to do everything that would result in complete and absolute disarray when it came to Mahisha's religious order. But how does one do that? Of course, she had planned it, but when she became a part of the system, she realised it was tougher than she had initially thought. It needed keener insight into what clicked inside people when they looked up at Mahisha.

Shukr had created a wonderful system. He had made long, bronze statues of Mahisha around the city where people could go and pray to him. He limited Mahisha's appearance in the streets, making him only show his face when necessary. He spread rumours amongst the people that Mahisha was a god and his powers came from Lord Brahma—that he was undefeatable. These rumours struck close to the hearts of the civilians who began to feel that a god walked amongst men.

But Mahisha was as much of a god as Indra was. They were both humans with exaggerated reputations. While Indra played on the love he received from his people, Mahisha played on fear. Shukr would spread lies such as if one didn't follow Mahisha, he would kill their child or wife. He would murder anyone who opposed him without even being in the same room. That fear was easy to haunt any ordinary civilian struck with poverty.

Like now.

The fear of Mahisha and his wrath had led more than a hundred civilians to stand in a long queue, holding jars of milk to do what Shukr called 'Doodh Abhishek'. To attain Mahisha's blessings, civilians had to pour milk at the feet of a fifty-feet tall statue of his so Mahisha would accept their prayers. But the problem was, the milk was the only thing these people would have had in their storage that would have filled their stomach. Instead, they were made to waste it like this. It was all false, of course, and why and how it started still eluded Gauri. Shukr wanted to build these customs, and once people began to follow them, it would feed into the larger myth of the god among men.

The tradition was flimsy. And Gauri had to be a part of it since she belonged to Shukr's entourage.

She had to stand with Airavati, close to the statue, and help the people in pouring the milk in the correct way. There were guards too, but they stood stoic and menacing, making sure no one broke the queue. The queue wound around all sides of the circular temple. Each person took their time and poured a jar of milk on the feet of Mahisha's statue. They chanted Mahisha's name. And then they left.

She knew the milk would go into the gutter, where it would go through some sort of cleaning process before it was served in the markets again for profit. It was a cycle. And it cut costs.

Gauri knew that today she had to act. Today was the way to do it. But how, was the question. Unlike other girls who worked under Durga who were given strict instructions, she was the only one who was told to follow her instincts and choose how to walk the right path.

And then she saw something that both melted her heart and made her blood boil.

Twelve years back, outskirts of Vindhya Range, ten miles from the Narmada River...

Gauri was in the swamp, screaming at the boy to help her. His name was Shashtri and he had let out a stick for her to grab on to, but the stick was purposefully far away. She tried to move forward, her legs stuck and frozen. Tears streamed down her face.

'Please...please...I beg you...' she cried.

But Shashtri just laughed with his friends.

'One thing will certainly come out. You aren't looking like a ghost who scares people anymore. You just look a tad bit ugly and extremely dirty,' Shashtri chuckled. He was two years older than her and a bully who had made it his life's mission to make her life a living hell.

'Please...please...' she begged. She felt the swamp closing in on her, engulfing her as she was about to swallow its murky waters.

And that was when she caught on to something that

was thrown at her. It was a rope. It felt like one. And she began to pull it towards herself.

She looked to see where it had come from and found that it was a man with a bald head and in a dark gown on the other side of the swamp. Seeing him, Shashtri scowled and scurried off with his friends deep into the woods.

She continued to pull herself on the rope and finally came out, drawing a deep breath and exhaling with a sigh of relief. She coughed and realised her clothes—her *only* clothes, which was just a pair of rags—were drenched in muddy swamp water. She looked up to see her saviour and the bald man greeted her with a smile. But he had skin latched onto his skull so tightly that it looked far too stretched for it to be comfortable. He had no brows and he looked strangely...different.

'What's your name, girl?'

'Gauri.'

'Who were those boys?'

She didn't answer, she was busy wiping the dirt.

'Where are your parents?' he asked.

'Dead.'

He raised his brows. 'You are an orphan?'

She nodded.

'I heard your cries from the camp,' he said. 'Do you want some buttered loaves? You must be famished.'

As an orphan, it was tough to trust anyone. Take Shashtri, for instance. He was an orphan too, as were his friends, and he had taken her inside his gang of thievery. They would steal from the folks in the villages and towns. Shashtri soon realised that she was doing better than him and his friends had begun to like her. So Shashtri turned on her and belittled her for her uncommon skin colour, he made her feel small, and relentlessly bullied her, because he was an insecure little brat.

'I would like that, yes,' she nodded. Though she wouldn't have the food, she could steal something and run away. But she was also grateful that the man had helped her.

'Good,' he smiled. 'Come.'

They walked back to his camp and she saw that it was a bunch of tents and all the men looked the same. Bald heads. Long black gowns. But some had black paint on their foreheads and throats, in the shape of strange symbols. It felt like, they were part of the cult. And they also had a lot of corpses that they carried with each other, wrapped in oilskins.

'What is this place?'

'A refuge,' he replied. 'We hide from the Asur.'

'Asur?'

'The demon of the south. Mahishasur,' the man said, as he gave her a piece of cloth to wipe her damp clothes with. He then made her sit down inside the tent while he brought loaves of bread with butter on it and curd on the side, and served it to her on a giant leaf.

She looked at the food. Was it poisoned? She didn't know. But her stomach gurgled and this was the best food she had eaten in a long time now. The man sat opposite to her, ramrod straight like a priest. And she guessed he was one, with all the amulets and the rings he wore.

'Are you a religious man?' she still asked.

He smiled. It was a plain, papery one. 'I worship the death and the afterlife. I perform the important rituals associated with death like antyeshi so I can send most people to moksha,' he paused. 'Aren't you going to eat?'

She looked again at the bread.

'You don't trust it.'

She didn't say anything.

'It's understandable. You have lived most of your life on the streets. It's tough to trust a bald man with a strange fascination towards death,' he grinned cheekily. 'Do you hate the boy who did this to you?'

She nodded. 'I can kill him.' She revealed her deepest frustration with gritted teeth. 'I can kill him for all the trouble he's caused me.'

'Why does he do it?'

'Because he's insecure.'

'And?'

'Because he hates how I look.'

'You look like that because there's an absence of melanin in your body,' the priest said. 'It's a skin pigmentation problem. Not your fault. It's just the way you were born.'

She smiled a shy smile. He had solved her biggest mystery. 'The spots began to come when I came on the streets.'

'I see,' he nodded. 'I hate bullies, Gauri. I have faced my share of bullies too when I was a child.'

She looked up, 'Okay.'

'And I always wanted to kill the ones who mentally abuse us.' He brought the knife in front of her. 'So, I give you the option.'

'To do what?' Her heart sped up.

'You told me you can kill him. So here it is,' he pushed the knife towards her.

'*Go and kill him.*'

The image of a poor boy with ribs more than skin close to his stomach was enough for her to feel something far worse. She felt she was there doing the job of a madman. The poor boy had a mug of milk and it would have been enough for him to sleep at night without a gurgling stomach. But instead, he was here to give the milk to a farcical statue that didn't even respect the sacrifice this young boy was making.

'No,' Gauri intervened. 'Go back.'

The boy was confused.

'You don't have to do it. GO!' she screamed at him.

The people behind him in the queue got confused. Airavati, who was by her side, was surprised.

'What are you doing?' she muttered under her breath.

'The right thing,' she clenched her jaw.

She came close to Mahisha's statue's feet and stood on it. Everyone was shocked that a mortal was standing like this on a god's feet and defiling it, but she started making an announcement before the guards caught on to her: 'You don't have to do this. This is wrong. The milk you waste is the very milk they sell back to you for more money. This doesn't give any goodwill to Mahisha. The king doesn't even know this is happening,' she screamed to the people. 'Everyone is making a fool of you. Do not get—'

The hilt of a sword was shoved into her abdomen, and she fell to the ground. Two soldiers had come, grunting because of the unexpected exertion. They kicked her and pierced her skin.

'You all have been fooled!' she kept screaming, blood pouring from her mouth. 'Do not listen...' she turned to Airavati. 'Convince the other slaves...this is not right...' and she faced the hilt again, on the face this time, her nose breaking as blood rushed down her nostrils.

There, lying on the ground, a smile appeared on her bloodied face.

'It's time to meet guruji for some discipline then, girl,' the guard said, picking her up and throwing her over his shoulder. 'You are speaking more than you are supposed to.'

She knew her punishment was going to be death. And she regretted letting her emotion get the better of her, but when she looked at the people—the ones who stared at her—she saw a glimmer of rebellion in their eyes. They were confused. They were...considering the possibility that she could be telling the truth.

And for that, she knew she was successful today.

Twelve years earlier...

Shashtri's shack was at the foot of the hill, close to the caves where the orphan-thieves had made themselves a little place to keep their loot.

She trudged forward, her little, dirty feet, trampling the grass.

The night had followed her and the sky was dark. Her eyes had begun to glow like that of a wolf. She moved seamlessly against the wind to reach the cave. She could hear the snores of her bullies. There were four of them. Three would be saved today.

Not Shashtri. He wouldn't live to see daybreak.

She tiptoed inside to find him. He slept like a child. He was a child. So was she. But Gauri was tired of this. She wanted to kill him. She could get the gang on her side then. They would follow her. They would listen to her. She could have a thriving career in thievery then. She could show the world that actions against her would have consequences. She was a threat, not a coward.

She brought the knife close to Shashtri's neck. Her breath came out forced. Her eyes twinkled with greed. With anger.

I have to do this.

The knife touched Shashtri's skin, but he didn't notice. He was still sleeping.

But do I want to do this?

With a heavy breath, she did what was important.

Twelve years earlier...

As the sun rose, he saw the girl again.

She had returned to the camp as he had expected. She still held his knife. And she walked with a clenched jaw and a face etched with worry.

He smiled at her. He hadn't slept the night before. He had not been sleeping for a while, as it was.

The girl knelt next to him and dropped the knife. She remained silent, letting the cawing of the ravens overtake the sound of silence.

'What happened?' he asked.

'I didn't kill him.'

He knelt down next to her and picked up the knife. 'Why?'

'Because it was not right.'

He nodded. 'Taking the life of a bully is not right? Is that so?'

She cut him a sharp look. Such fire in an eight-year-old was a sight for the old man's sore eyes. He almost chuckled with enthusiasm.

'If I do that, then I'll be just like him. In fact, worse.'

Such wisdom.

'Yes,' the man said. 'An important lesson you have learnt today, girl. Hurting someone else is the easiest thing to do. But sparing them from that hurt needs a whole new level of talent. And fortunately, you possess it,' he tossed the knife in the corner. 'Do you want to be part of something more than just this pettiness? Do you want to be part of a revolution?'

She was confused. It was tempting.

'You have the fire that I seek. Join me,' he offered her his hand.

'To do what?'

'To be with Durga.'

She arched her brows, 'Who is she?'

'You will know soon enough, and when you do, your life will change.'

She contemplated. 'I can have that loaf of bread now, I suppose.'

He smiled, 'Sure. Go in the tent. It's been laid out for you.'

She got up and started walking inside, but then stopped. She turned back and asked him: 'What is your name?'

She was warming up to him. 'My birth name has no significance anymore.'

'What should I call you then?'

'Yama,' he said. 'Just Yama.'

10

On the day his wife had been kidnapped, Tamar had been excruciatingly busy.

He hadn't had the time to address Bashkala who had been waiting outside with urgent business. But for Tamar, work had always been top priority and he didn't let anyone interfere with it.

He was sitting with scrolls and papers laid out in front of him, looking over them. The jivagribha, a law enforcement officer of the district, was next to him. They were on the carpet, legs crisscrossed, their eyes darting over the papers.

'By the sea storms and seashells!' he exclaimed under his breath. 'Who would do something like that?' he looked up at the officer.

'A bunch of privileged brats, children of our ministers,' said the officer.

He was reading the report the officer had given. As the Prime Minister, his job wasn't just overlooking the economy and the administration, but also looking over the judiciary and the execution of its decisions in the state, especially during the absence of the king. The court was his and he had the right to extend justice in whatever way he deemed fit and just.

Obviously, it was based on public opinion.

The report was on how a woman had been found. She was alive. But she was badly disfigured. Beaten. Bruised and raped.

'A farmer's daughter,' he said, under his breath.

'Yes. The men just sort of had a liking for her. She didn't respond to their advances. Seems like they didn't take no for an answer.'

Tamar couldn't believe how much violence towards women had increased, especially because Mahisha perpetuated it under his leadership. He would display casual cruelty towards women. 'Where are the men right now?'

'In their houses, my lord.'

He couldn't believe it. 'And why aren't they in prison?'

'Because...his highness wouldn't like it if I locked his ministers' progeny, my lord.'

It was true.

'So...will we have a trial for this?'

'We have to,' he sighed. 'Otherwise this is a rebellion waiting to happen. The women do most of the weaving and the moulding of pottery among other important work. We can't lose their labour'

'But will you convict the men?'

Tamar knew that answer very well. He simply couldn't. Mahisha would not allow it. This was the kingdom where men roamed free and women faced whatever was meted out to them. Tamar's wife had often protested. Thankfully, she was safe, but that was also because she was his wife.

'Set up the trial three days from now.'

The officer nodded.

Tamar went to the door and there he saw Bashkala with his thick, wavy mane, waiting with concern over his face. His eyes were stark with dread and worry.

'What happened?' Tamar asked.

For a moment, Bashkala didn't know what to say, but then he coughed up the courage to speak...

Twelve years earlier...

Charini laid next to the man she had just killed. He was an old man who he had lifted his dhoti and had tried to force himself on her. But the bloody rock was in her hand and she was shivering. She had never killed someone. She was just eight years old. She couldn't believe what she'd just done and as she turned her head, she saw the man's smashed head. Her heart was beating fast.

Then she saw someone in front through her blurry vision.

'Charini, are you okay? Are you fine?' he began to shake her, and she felt her vison clear a bit.

'Y-y-yes.'

'What have you done?' her brother looked at the corpse next to her. 'It was a gramani you just killed.'

'He was doing nasty things to me,' she said.

His brother quietened. 'I am sorry. I am so sorry you faced this.' He hugged her tightly. 'You did well. But we need to run now. You have killed a village headman. We cannot stay here anymore. We have to escape.'

He carried her in his arms.
And they went deep into the forest.
She was glad he was there for her.

It was the afternoon of the second day of the Nine Nights when Charini saw everything was in disarray. She was standing close to the fountain in a static pose, ready to reveal the great discovery.

But she had to choose her time well. Tamar had not found his wife, for obvious reasons, but he had sent hundreds of men to different parts of the kingdom by now and was sitting anxiously on the ground, cursing himself. There were other guards in the complex, with the cooks and maids of the palace, whispering in fear and hoping Sulochna was fine.

Bashkala came next to her and whispered: 'You shouldn't have left her hand.'

'Again, I tell you, she is not a child. She was right there, captain.'

Bashkala growled. 'I don't trust you, girl. You are a devious little shit, aren't you? I know you had something to do with it.'

'What do you even mean? Why would I have anything to do with this?'

'Because look at your face. You have no remorse or longing for your mistress. It's like you don't care.'

She did have an aloof, placid expression.

Charini frowned. *You are probably right.*

'DID YOU FIND HER?' Tamar shouted, to intervene

in between. 'Instead of quarrelling, the two of you should go out and find her!'

'My lord, we have searched all the four sides. No one has seen her.'

'How is it possible?' Tamar came on his feet, his headpiece dangling from one side of his forehead. He was a short, stumpy man with the look of a bear. 'How does a woman disappear in thin air? Someone at the market must have seen her. Charini!' he exclaimed. 'Did you happen to see her or not? What happened there?' He was shaking in excitement and seemed almost on the verge of a breakdown because he had asked her the same question multiple times.

'My lord, I wanted to let you know something,' she said.

'What? What?'

Bashkala grinned. He thought she was going to confess. But instead, she handed Tamar the scroll.

'I found it at the eastern gate, delicately tucked in the bushes, my lord, as if it wanted us to find it. I was planning to give it to you, but Captain Bashkala was blaming everything on me, so I was a little shaken.'

'What is it?' He practically snatched the scroll out of her hands.

'My lord,' she began, 'it's a letter from the kidnapper.'

His expression changed. Almost taken aback. A little hopeful too.

He unfurled and read it:

I write with hope to you, my love. Yes, it's me. Sulochna. I want you to know the he has kept me safe. He is not hurting me. He just wants you to do something for him. He wants you to...

His eyes widened at the request and then he stopped reading and looked at Charini. 'You had this and you didn't tell me for an hour?' he fumed.

'I didn't know if it was real or not, my lord.'

'It's her bloody handwriting!' He threw the scroll on the floor. 'The madman wants me to do the impossible, and only then will he free her.'

'What does he want?' Bashkala asked. 'You should not give in to any monetary demands. We will find her, my lord,' he promised solemnly.

'It's not money,' he shook his head, sounding slightly defeated.

'Then?' the captain stepped forward in confusion.

'He will only free her,' he shuddered, 'if I execute four men.'

'Four men? Who are these men?'

He looked up at Charini and Bashkala. 'They are the rapists, captain. They are the rapists and if I execute them—I will have the fury of Mahisha and the rebellion of the men in this city to deal with.'

12 years earlier...

Few months later, Charini had come to terms with the fact that she had killed a man, and while bile rose at the back of the throat at the thought, she willed herself to walk from one village to another. They were fugitives. They already had been poor, but her brother was working at the village office while they were earlier stationed. He would bring food for her. But now, ever since she had killed the headman, they were on the run.

'I'm hungry, anna,' she said.

He didn't say anything. He was quiet. She was following him. Tripping. Staggering and moving forward.

'You shouldn't have killed him,' he said, after a while.

'But nasty—'

'You could have hurt him,' he cut her off sharply and turned to her, ferociously angry. 'You could have hit him right between his bloody legs. But you killed him!'

She could see he was angry and she felt like crying. Anna, if angry, was not kind to her.

'I had a nice fucking job, Charini. Everything is gone. You are a killer. And I am assisting a killer.'

'You don't mean that.'

He didn't say anything further. He was not supposed to be rude. He was her brother. He was the only man she could ever trust.

And then he turned. His eyes softened. 'I'm sorry.' He stood in front of her. The sun was high and they were stuck between endless trees. Sweating. They'd been in the same clothes for days now. Surviving on berries and other things foraged from the forest. 'I shouldn't have said that. I'm hungry too, and I'm just frustrated.'

She nodded. She didn't say anything.

So they carried on. On their way, they happened to find a small camp and Anna saw the food that was being cooked there.

'I should see if we can get something from there.'

'Are you going to ask them?'

'No,' he shook his head.

'Steal? But isn't stealing bad?'

'Well, my dear sister, I think that boat has already sailed. We are too deep in this now.'

And he did.

Little did she know that that was the last time she would be seeing him.

Charini knew that he had tried attacking the camp but when she learnt it belonged to King Mahisha's people, she was afraid. She had seen her brother getting stabbed in the stomach and bleeding out. And when she had cried out for help, her cries were met with silence. Then, a hand had grabbed her from behind.

That was when she met the kindest man she had ever known. An Arya. A Deva. The priest king, Agni, who performed rituals around the element of fire. He had seen her alone and had seen she was quite small and needed his help. He had given her food and had tended to her.

After that night, she was not the same person. She had killed someone and because of her hunger, she had let her brother die too. She couldn't feel anything. Agni Dev had helped her a lot through the process and made her work under Durga. Learn a lot of things. Strategies, especially.

She was in the room, glad that the plan was going well. Everything was well. Tamar had bought her story of her finding the letter outside. The handwriting gave it away. And as she was sitting on the cot, thinking about her next plan of action, there was a knock on the door.

She went to open it, only to see the stark, dark eyes of Bashkala.

'What do you want?' she spoke in a mellow tone.

'To talk.'

'About what?'

'My men were outside the eastern gate and they saw no bloody scroll. You were lying. You wrote it yourself. Forged it, perhaps. You are a scholar, aren't you?'

She was, indeed. Agni had taught her all about geography, history and science. She was learned. 'You have no proof.'

'My gut feeling is the proof.'

'Well, tell that to Prime Minister Tamar then.'

He clenched his jaw. 'I know you, Charini. I know you more than you think I do.'

'And how is that?'

For a moment, there was a flicker of fear in his eyes, like he wanted to say something, but then he just pulled up his tunic. Charini looked down. She noticed a long, burnt scar. And her eyes looked sharply up, back at his face. Realisation began to dawn.

'No,' she whispered, and for the first time in many years, remnants of emotions began to surface on her face.

'Yes, Charini,' he said. 'It's me. Your anna.'

11

Chandra was prepared when the Admiral called her for a meeting late at night.

The boat was rocking. And she was in the cellar. Bottles and jars of drinks were kept in different places. She pulled one of them out and made sure no one was there. Glancing around, she pulled a vial from the pocket of her tunic she was wearing and poured the constituents inside the bottle. It was crushed hemlock mixed with water that she had been carrying around throughout the time she was on board.

It was supposed to kill the Admiral. Slow and steady. No froth. It'd look like the man's heart simply stopped beating. But as she stood there with the bottle, her heart yelped and screamed. The Admiral was a good man.

But...

She had a mission.

Licking her lips, she thought back to where it had all begun for her. Why she had joined Durga...

5 years earlier, Lothal Port, modern-day Gujarat...

Lothal was a thriving centre of trade and commerce. The Sabarmati river acted as an instrument of economy, as it flew right towards Africa and other continents where the export and import business was perfect. The entire port was covered in a mud brick wharf where the ships would be docked. There was a tower right in the middle of the port, high up, where the gramani was stationed. There were dockyards for the ships, and warehouses made of sun-dried bricks for the cargo to be placed.

Lothal was also popular for jewellery and Chandra was a beadmaker. She had a small shack close to the wharf, near the market of other beadmakers. She made cheap jewellery out of the seashells she collected, as well as stones and pebbles, hoping it would sell.

She had survived alone as an orphan for the longest time. Her mother had died a few years back. She used to sit at the shop earlier. Lothal was a quiet economic centre where no one troubled anyone. And the best part was, there were no battles here. Lothal was so important that the Aryas and the Dasas found ways to collaborate over it and found a middle ground. The gramani was a staunch man and he made sure bad blood didn't flow into the port's waters.

On days when the Dasas did their business, the Aryas didn't. And since the Aryas had gone into hiding for a while, the Dasas were the ones who conducted business here the most.

Like today.

The sun was glimmering over the waters and the wind was chilly. She saw the local plava docked and the flag hoisted over it had a buffalo's sign. She knew it meant that it belonged to Mahisha. The men had come out, except the black-armoured soldiers, but there was one specific man she had her eyes on. He was a young lad with crystal grey eyes and a charming smile. He was embracing the gramani who had come out to welcome them. A crowd had gathered to watch. The man's skin was bronze and perfect.

'Who is he?' she asked the boy who was playing with her beads. His name was Bikram, a local porter. Even though half the size of a normal man and just ten years in age, he would carry as much luggage as his meagre body would allow.

'Sanghrihitri,' he said.

'What?' she was confused.

'A treasurer in King Mahisha's court.'

'A treasurer?'

He was moving up towards the tower in the middle of the citadel, where the priests would worship their gods and perform rituals of all kinds. All the people were huddled there, standing in awe, as if he was some king or a prince. But then Lothal was a place where natives would appreciate outsiders and even treat them with deference, especially the moneymaker of Mahisha's kingdom.

Mahisha had slowly grown to become an emperor and he had taken his time. He had attacked places. He had looted and plundered, but he was always respectful towards a lot of other places where he was supposed to be respectful. Like Lothal. He was not a vicious man. Or at least, that's what his men proclaimed.

'Why is he here?' she asked.

'A trade deal of sorts. Exclusivity for Mahisha's ships for few years,' the boy said, and then he shrugged. 'Heard from some soldiers who had heard talk among the maids back in the tower,' he paused. 'But the gramani will refuse, of course. I mean, he would never let anyone be exclusive in these lands, at least.'

It was all hearsay, so she didn't take it seriously.

'Did you eat anything today?' she asked the boy.

He was still distracted so Chandra slapped him on the head.

'Yeah, yeah, I did.'

'What did you have?'

He scratched his head. 'Umm...rice?'

She slapped him on the head again. 'Why don't you eat? Don't I give you money? What do you do with that?' She had been helping Bikram for a while now. She thought of him as a brother. But he was just one naughty little kid.

'Um...I...um...waste it?' he was trying to find excuses.

She sighed. She gave him another coin. 'Please go and have something to eat.'

He nodded and rushed off.

Pursing her lips, she sat down and tried to sell her beads to the foreigners and natives. Soon it was nightfall, and when she was closing her shack, she realised she was the last of them. The shore was empty. The wharf was isolated. Covering the shack with a cloth, she moved for the streets when her eyes caught on to the glimmering fire torches inside the Durmukha's oakwood ship. There were people on it. Their whispers were audible.

Didn't all soldiers from the ship go to the tower?

She had definitely seen many following Durmukha. She moved closer to the ship and peered in from the corner of the glass window in the lower quarter of the deck, only to see more than fifty soldiers, all huddled together in the kitchen of the ship.

'When the sun rises, we need to ignite the bloody place. And attack,' the man in the middle said. 'Burn the place down, so King Mahisha can rebuild it and make it his own.'

No.

For a moment, she was stunned.

And then she knew, what she had to do.

Find Bikram.

They were laughing.

She was in the captain's lodge, and the bottle was in the middle. The Admiral was wearing a long shawl, covering his inked body, as he sat on the opposite side of the table.

'You did well battling that Greek ship, girl,' he said.

She smiled, bowing dramatically. 'Well, you taught me.'

'I never thought you would reach where you are. When you had come, you were a cook. You impressed me always and here you are. Look at you, a boatswain.'

'I don't plan to be that much longer,' she smiled.

'Of course you don't,' he said, as he picked up the wine and poured it for her and himself, keeping the bottle right back where it was. 'Utharaka, my dear quartermaster, is an old bird. He's a good man though. He's loyal. And that's important. What do you think, girl? Are you loyal?' he twirled his moustache when he asked her. The cup right next to his mouth. He didn't drink though.

She was biting her lips in stress. She wanted to take the poisoned drink away from him, but she didn't. She was...confused.

She was supposed to poison him. And then pretend that it was an accident. She was supposed to make him write a fake letter in which he would say that she was to be the captain now. It was a successor letter for her. So when he died, she could command the ship and bring it towards the ship that was sailing from Ceylon. Attack it.

But she was overthinking. She didn't want the Admiral to die. Perhaps, she could convince him.

'I am loyal, captain.'

'I think you are,' he said with a proud smile.

'Why don't you ever reveal your name?'

He shrugged. 'A name is not important. We are just shadows left in this world. Our titles are what we should go with.'

'You were an admiral before you became...'

'A legal pirate?' he chuckled. 'Yes, I was. I worked with the Devas. Closely functioned around dear old Indra.'

She raised her brows. He worked with the Devas? That was not part of the debriefing she had received before being sent undercover here.

'And then one day I decided to resign. The Devas weren't happy. I was their prized possession after all. So, they forced me.'

'Why did you want to resign?'

'Oh well, I was frustrated with their conquests across the foreign lands and what not. They wanted to expand their trade. Moreover, I wanted to be with my family.'

'You have a family?'

There was a flicker of pain in his eyes, as he took the drink and finally sipped on it.

Her heart went berserk and began to thump harder than ever. She wanted to scream and her eyes were marked with fright.

He took another sip.

The damage was done. She had to ask him to write a letter now. She didn't have time. Not anymore.

'They killed my family,' he said.

'Who?'

'The Devas. They didn't want me to resign, so they killed them and blamed it on someone. I learnt of this much later and I left them, joined Mahisha and now do what he says,' he sighed. 'Oh, by the gods of water, this taste different. Don't you think?'

She licked her lips. Was that why the Devas wanted her to poison the Admiral? Because he had betrayed them? Because killing a good man like him didn't make sense.

Have I been manipulated by my employers?

But she had to stick to her plan. Her mission. Durga was not like the Devas. She was different. She had to tell him he had been poisoned and that he had to write a successor letter. Only then would she give him the antidote. But there was no antidote. It was a lie. She was holding on to a vial which had the fake antidote. It was just plain water.

'I called you here because I wanted to give you this,' he said, as a terrible cough took over him. He handed her a scroll. 'Open it. Gods, I feel stuffy. But...' he had begun to sweat, but he was still grinning.

She unfurled the scroll and saw what was written.

I write this in full consciousness and hope. I hereby declare Chandra Ghata to be the Captain of this ship.

Yours dearly,
Samudra

12 years earlier...

She tried to find him in the dead of night. She tried her hardest. But he was nowhere to be seen. Bikram had vanished. She had gone to his nest, where he usually resided with other porter friends of his, but they had not seen him either.

By the time she was exhausted and ready to give up, she realised the sun was coming up.

She had no time.

I am sorry, Bikram.

And she left the port. She took the nearest reed boat, stole it, and set sail on the Sabarmati river, moving for another port, but she was tired and she needed rest.

It was only a day later, when she walked into the other towns and villages, did she hear about the massacre in Lothal. Everyone had died.

And the guilt of leaving those people behind...

She had become selfish. She had thought only about herself. The guilt was killing her.

After that day, she had tried to find someone to oppose Mahisha. Her search ahd brought her to Varuna's camp. Varuna was a popular priest-king who handled the naval network of the Devas. And she told him about what she had done. He was happy that someone had come to him and was honest about the regret. He told her to work with Durga, so she could get a shot at redemption and save many lives like that of Bikram's.

But seeing the scroll in front of her she shivered and asked: 'I am...but...I'm a...'

'Don't say that you are a woman. I don't give a rat's ass...' he stopped and coughed again, 'if you are a woman or a man. You did well and it's time for me to sit back and relax.'

'Samudra...that's...I know...'

'Yes. I'm one of the Devas,' he smiled and tried to come up from his chair and walk around. 'I was Varuna's brother. Half-brother, to be precise. He wasn't kind to me.'

'I'm sorry,' she was weeping.

'What happen—' he collapsed on the ground, his body shaking violently.

She grabbed hold of him. She was trying to help him, but she knew he was going to die. 'He told me you were bad...he told me...I didn't know...I...' She was blurting out fragments of words which didn't make sense.

The Admiral gave a final flash of sympathy, a flash of shock to her, and then he closed his eyes as his soul departed his body. He remained there, in her arms, as she cried on his unmoving chest.

She didn't know who to trust. Who not to.

She had killed a good man.

To further a greater cause of dharma.

She joined this revolution to get rid of regret. But instead, she got more of it.

I hope this is worth it, Durga.

12

Alliances between two large groups are often common and complicated at the same time. One has to understand what the other person wants and at the same time put forth the conditions that one oneself desires. Then the two groups try to find a middle ground which makes them happy, and each group is left with something they want.

One has to have a certain way to talk to people. And observe their body language. Their facial expressions.

Unfortunately, where Mahisha was sitting—in front of the hearth inside the large tent, opposite Thamisada—it was impossible to see his face.

Mahisha was alone. He didn't need Trinetra here. Not for speaking. But he stood guard outside.

He could see there was a certain awkward body language Thamisada was carrying. Little awkward. Little frustrated. He wasn't comfortable.

'What is it?' Mahisha asked. 'Is it Durga?'

The last time he had known she was here, he had brushed it away. It was stupid. No one could see the future he knew, but he had to be pragmatic about it.

'How can you enter into this alliance with her outside, Mahisha?' Thamisada asked.

'Because she's not here.'

Rigoli snapped, 'I saw her.'

Yeah. Mahisha sighed. 'My men have searched all

your men and your men searched mine. We didn't see anything out of order. There's no one in particular that raises suspicion. Frankly, Rigoli, I believe you saw wrong.'

'I never see wrong,' the priest said with an annoyed, offended grimace.

'Can we focus on the job at hand? I will leave after that, once this is complete, and you don't have to worry about Durga.'

'What really astounds me, Mahisha, is that I have always loved wars. Battles. They happened in front of me. But shadows, Mahisha, shadows are the most dangerous. They come from behind you, follow you, and they can stab you. That's why I hate assassins.'

The king of Maisuru nodded. 'You are right. I have had attempts at assassinations on myself before.'

'I'm sure. You are an important man,' Thamisada sighed. 'Fine. Let's discuss.'

'Good,' Mahisha grinned. He drew out the scrolls and laid them in front of the chief to show to him. 'I am ready to offer you two thousand gold bars and a piece of land.'

'Which piece of land?'

'The one you sit on.'

He raised his head. Impressed. 'Interesting.'

'Yes. I thought it would be nice for you to see the land you will own.'

'And in return you want...'

'Your loyalty.' Mahisha filled his goblet with wine, his legs crisscrossed, sitting on the ground. 'I want you to be a part of my army and help me destroy the remnants of Aryas.'

'You want to wipe out Aryas from the face of Jambudvipa?'

'Yes. The Devas still hold power in few areas. You go and kill them. Simple,' he smiled.

'You treat us...you treat us like paid mercenaries, Mahisha?' he growled. 'Do you think we are mercenaries? We are...what? Labourers of violence for you?'

Mahisha could see he was offended. Rigoli was frowning too. The Panas were a proud race and they didn't like if someone behaved unjustly towards them. He sipped from his spiced wine and said, 'Of course not. You have been offered more than any other ally of mine.'

'A nomadic community like ours doesn't need land,' he shifted the scroll back to Mahisha. 'The bars of gold don't mean anything to us because we work on war bounty and barter.' He shoved the rest of the scroll towards Mahisha.

For a moment, Mahisha contemplated. *What should I do?* He wished Shukr were here to flash his greasy grin and manipulate the situation in his favour. That's what he did.

'You humiliate us by giving us such petty offers. And I thought we were building a friendship,' the chief scoffed.

'Of course we are.'

'Good,' Thamisada came on his feet. 'Why don't I offer you something?'

'Offer me what?'

He walked to the flaps of the tent and gave out an order in his native tongue. A girl entered. Young.

Beautiful. Exotic. She had honey-coloured eyes. Golden. She was decked in elaborate jewellery and a gown.

'This is Tabiti.'

Mahisha came up on his feet and wished her.

'She's my daughter.'

Oh. Mahisha gritted his teeth. He knew where this was going.

'Why don't you marry her, and I shall do what you want me to do?'

Mahisha considered this. He looked at the girl again. The girl had no problem. She was okay. If she were a wench, he would have bedded her. But she was a princess and she was supposed to be respected. Mahisha had one rule. It was one rule that he never broke in the decades of warmongering he had done—he never married anyone to form alliance. He had his reasons.

'I can't,' he said. 'Tabiti seems nice. But I can't marry her.'

'And why is that?'

He paused. He didn't want to go. Plus, he felt the urge to drink some of the Soma milk again. He knew he hadn't liked those visions, but they had somehow comforted him, now that he thought about it. Just swimming in the past.

'We can discuss it tomorrow.'

'For sure, Mahisha. Take your time,' Thamisada came close and he smelled of charcoal to Mahisha. 'It's just a marriage. You don't have to worry.'

It's more complicated than that.

There was no feast that night. And there was no one else in the tent. He didn't want anyone.

He had the goat's milk mixed with Soma in his hand, disregarding Trinetra's warnings about indulging in it. He sat down and looked at the plain, white milk and then he drank it all in a quick gulp. For a moment, he felt nothing. But he was prepared for all sorts of visions and trances he would get this time.

He closed his eyes.

I'm ready.

He waited. And he waited. But nothing happened. He opened his eyes, annoyed, when he realised he was no more in the tent. He was in a garden. An orchid field, to be exact. The skies were filled with seagulls. And he knew this scenario. He knew where he was.

No. Not here.

'I hate it when you go into this thought process of yours,' a voice came from the side.

No.

He turned to see her. That face. It was so real, he wanted to touch it. She had the most beautiful black hair, so deep and rich, light brown eyes, and a smile that would always ignite fire in him.

'Varya,' he whispered, 'you are...'

'Alive? Of course I am.' She was running her fingers through his hair.

'But how?'

'Don't worry about that. How have you been doing?'

'Bad. I miss you.'

'Do you?' she asked, with genuine interest.

Of course he did. He missed her. He had met her

when he had become a part of Shukr's tutelage. He used to go to the fish market to meet her often. She would sell him salmon and smile at him. Slowly, he began to spend time with her. He used to gather lots of cherries so he could gift them to her. He loved her like his father perhaps never loved his mother. For that, he was proud of himself.

'Do you remember how we planned our marriage?'

'Yes. You wanted to do it on a ship. Right in the middle of the sea.'

'Yes, I did. And wear jewellery made of conch shells. I was stupid,' she chuckled. 'You were thinking of leaving Shukr too, right?'

He nodded. He didn't want any part in fighting the Aryas. He had found his purpose. It was to make her happy.

'Then you didn't have to kill me, Mahisha,' she said, her eyes tearing up.

'But I was…I never married. I kept that promise.'

'How does it matter? You killed me.'

Flashes of that memory floated before his eyes.

No.

He didn't want to remember it, but it was right there. He had seen her talking to a boy. For a moment, he had thought she was in love with someone else, but when he peered and listened—

'You were spying on me. You were sent by the Devas because they knew someone like Shukr was stirring problems.'

She nodded. 'I was doing my job. But I had begun to love you.'

'No you didn't,' he said through gritted teeth.

'Alright fine,' she grinned. 'I didn't.'

He remembered that day. He had confronted her. And she had said the same thing that she was saying now, with a vicious smile on her face:

'Did you really think I would marry you, you green-skinned ogre? Have you seen your ugly face? You are more disgusting than the shit I stepped on today.'

He grabbed her by the neck and pushed her down. And began to choke her. But there was no struggle. She was not affected at all.

In fact, she was laughing.

'I loved you and you betrayed me.'

'Is that why you hate women? Huh? Huh?'

He wanted to squeeze her neck more. Tighter. Tighter.

Until he heard a voice. A different one. Not Varya's. But softer, and his vision began to blur. He saw his hands were wrapped around the golden-eyed Tabiti's neck.

And he left the grasp.

She was choking and had gone red.

'What are you doing here?' he scampered to the side and searched for his blade, but he couldn't find it.

She massaged her throat. 'I wanted to meet you,' she sputtered. 'You were murmuring. I wanted to...'

'What do you want?' he rasped.

'Are you okay?'

He was sweating profusely, his eyes had gone bloodshot, and his skin felt feverish. 'Yeah, yeah I am...'

'Calm down, my lord,' she came close, trying to touch his feet but he slapped it away.

'Stay where you are. Did Thamisada send you?'

She shook her head. 'I was smitten by how good you looked that I sneaked out of my tent to meet you, to try and convince you to make sure the marriage takes place.'

He narrowed his eyes. 'Don't fucking lie. I know you are lying. Your kind always does. I am a green-skinned monster for you all,' he was rambling now.

'Monster? I don't think so,' she moved forward, trying to touch his feet again and this time, he didn't move.

So she massaged his feet, slowly tracing her fingers upwards to his muscled arms. 'You have a very poor opinion of yourself, your highness.'

Mahisha wouldn't have cared if it were any other girl, but Tabiti seemed suspicious. Why would she come here? What were her intentions? Did Thamisada send her to spy on him? But why? He had nothing to offer, no intelligence of any kind.

'Calm down, your highness,' she pressed his arms. 'Did you have my father's stupid milk? You shouldn't drink that. It's harmful for your brain.'

He pursed his lips and hugged his legs to his chest.

'What did you see?'

'Huh?'

'You were having a vision, weren't you?'

'I...' he didn't want to tell her. 'Can you leave?'

'I can. But I am requesting you to rethink your refusal of the marriage.'

'Why? You are young. Why do you want to marry me?'

She had an excited grin on her face. 'Because I have heard about you so much. You are honourable and you have valour...and you are powerful. Who wouldn't want to marry you?'

She had a childlike quality.

During his earlier alliances where marriage was offered, the girls had never had the guts to come and meet him like this. But Tabiti was different. She had dimples when she smiled, and she was excited to see him. *Him*. An ogre.

'I shouldn't have come,' she said, after a brief silence. 'But I hope you reconsider it. I was against the idea of marriage until I knew my father was thinking of marrying me off to you. I mean, there's no better partner for me, I believe.'

She came on her feet and began to move for the flaps. She turned back. Mahisha looked up. She wanted to say something, but she refrained. And then she left. He was left there alone. Confused.

But most of all, he felt good about himself.

Something he hadn't felt in a long time.

13

The following day, when he reached the outpost, Seksh felt something was off about the place.

He was at the outskirts of the outpost. About a hundred yards away. Hundred men behind him. Asiloma, his lover and his lieutenant, was by his side, mounted on his horse. And they looked at the empty fort which was on an elevated piece of land. There was no sign of Durga or her army or even a tiger anywhere close by. He had sent his scouts to all the four corners of the outpost, and they had all returned in one piece.

'General, we didn't see any footprints of any kind. I don't think there is anyone here,' one of the scouts said and everyone chimed in to agree.

Seksh shared a worried glance with Asiloma. The man was gorgeous. Curly locks of hair falling just over his face, a defined jaw line, and nice dark eyes. He had a mole on one side of his mouth. Seksh had started liking him quite early on, when he had seen him as just a soldier. He had made sure he got closer to him.

'Is she playing with us?' Asiloma asked.

'Probably,' Seksh sighed. 'But I am not someone who will get played. Secure the perimeter. First squad—east.' And then he directed all the cavalry squads to surround the lush greenery where the outpost stood. They were going to be the first line of defence. The archers were the second. And then the infantry moved closer, along with Seksh and Asiloma.

Once his men had finally formed a tight-knit system around the outpost—he waited for some action to start. Someone to attack. Some loud, shrill call. Something.

But there was nothing.

He could only hear the cawing of ravens and the smell of cherries and apples from the groves.

'We should move in,' Seksh said finally. 'I believe I was wrong.'

'About what?' asked a confused Asiloma.

'That this is an ambush. It's not an ambush. It's a waste of my fucking time,' he snarled as he thumped his stallion on the side and began to move further in.

He reached the wooden gates of the outpost, his long cape flowing in the back, a flag with the buffalo insignia dangling from the saddle. He had leather gloves on and he was wearing a silver breastplate, kneepads, and large, black boots. Seksh could only see from one of his eyes. The other was marble. It would move like a realistic eye, but he had no vision there.

He dismounted from the horse and pulled out his sword. Ordinarily he should have let his guards open the door, but he had to set an example of bravery. Plus, the perimeter was well protected. Any surprise attack from any of the directions would be well taken care of.

He banged on the door first. And stepped back.

No response.

He looked back at Asiloma. Sweat beads trickled down his forehead. He banged on the door again.

Bloody hell.

He didn't wait. With a quick shove of his legs, he kicked the door open. It flung apart and his foot landed on the muddy floor. His body stiffened automatically, poised for a fight, and with the sword up high, he waited for a sudden attack by someone.

Silence.

Then he stepped closer, his guards following him, entering with their bows and arrows, ready to attack anyone.

His eyes darted towards something though, as he entered the middle of the outpost. Someone was sitting crosslegged on the ground. The person's eyes were closed. She was scarred. Her hair was in a perfect braid. She didn't care that someone had just barged in.

Seksh motioned for his men to check the entire outpost for any surprise attacks, while he casually strolled over to the girl. As his shadow loomed over her. Finally, she opened her eyes, a smile spreading on her face.

'Are you Durga?' he asked, chuckling at the incredulous sight in front of him. He couldn't make sense of the situation.

She nodded. Her smile widened. 'Yes, I am. Thank you so much, General Seksh for paying me a visit.'

Seksh got himself comfortable in the captain's room of the outpost. It was a small, dull four-walled place, with a grilled window overlooking the forest. There was a short table and a cushion to sit on. He looked at the scrolls and the papers to see what the captain was supposed to be doing before he was savagely murdered by the woman. And the only sound was of a leaking pipe. Tip. Tip. Tip.

Asiloma was in the room too, just staring out of the window.

'So, we are not leaving?' he asked.

'Till I know about her intentions, we're not going anywhere.'

'Why?'

'We have just arrived. Give it time. Rest here. Also, it's an outpost. I am sending a messenger to bring backup forces, so they can station themselves here. Till that time, we have to sit tight and hope everything is just dandy.'

'She's making you think,' Asiloma ran his fingers through his curly hair.

'Yes she is, that bitch,' he leaned back. 'Either she's crazy or damn smart. I'm yet to figure out which.'

'Well, let's hope she's the former.'

'No sign of the tiger, right?'

'The scouts were sent out. No backup. Nothing. This woman has guts. I can tell you that.'

'She can have all the bloody bravery she wants. But Mahisha wants her alive. He wants to meet her personally. I think he will gut her like a pig when he meets her.'

Asiloma didn't say anything. He kissed Seksh on the forehead and then moved to the door. 'I'm sending her in. Take care.'

Seksh smiled at his lover and nodded. He waited for Durga for a moment or two. He was a bit hesitant. The girl was raising the hair on the back of his neck.

But he remained static as she entered. She walked in, iron clasps around her wrists. A guard who was behind her made her stand. Seksh relieved the soldier and he left.

They both stared at each other in silence. He studied her eyes, mouth and her skin. She was dark brown in colour and had the most striking eyes—they shone brightly like a tiger's.

'So, you are the one who had killed my entire outpost?' he asked condescendingly.

'I am, indeed.' It was maddening how calm she was.

'What you have done counts as offence against the state,' he paused, reining in his emotions. 'I'm here. You wanted me to capture you. And I have. So I suppose, everything is going according to the plan.'

'What plan? I'm bound in chains. I'm in no position to have a plan.'

He chuckled, sipping from his goblet. 'Don't play games with me, woman. I have battled through campaigns you have no idea of. I have killed thousands of enemies on the ground who have tried to outsmart me. There's a reason why I'm the General of the strongest empire these lands have seen. So don't you dare play games with me.'

'I'm not,' she shrugged.

He was getting agitated. He sipped more wine to calm his nerves. 'So there was no plan?'

She was silent. And then she asked, 'Can I take a sip?'

'What?' Sheksh was baffled.

'Of the wine you are drinking.'

He arched his brows. What sorcery was this? With

a deep, unsettled sigh, he walked to her, glass in hand, and offered her the drink. She took it and had a sip of it.

'Ah, my throat. It was parched,' she smiled.

'So, what is it? What are you hiding? What's your plan?'

'I thought there would be more torture. I expected instruments and blades. I had mentally prepared myself for it,' she laughed.

She was joking. She wasn't taking this seriously. That unnerved him. Here she was, a chit of a girl, and she displayed no fear in front of a mongrel.

'Fine, I'll tell you.'

He waited.

She continued:

'Someone will die today.'

The soldier was tired. Exhausted. The heat was killing and as nice as the armour looked on people, they were pretty heavy to carry, made of heavy iron as they were. He tried to pull the flaps and pushed down his pyjamas to take a piss.

But he didn't notice the shadow. It was coming from the east. Moving towards him. The shadow had one more thing. A knife. It moved for the soldier. Quick as a whip.

Stabbing him in the neck with precision. The knife turned and twisted. Blood sprayed. His body lay partially naked on the ground. Eyes popping out.

The killer moved away. Wiping the blood from the knife.

As if nothing happened.

'What do you mean?' Seksh asked.

'One of your men will die,' she replied slowly, as if explaining something to a child.

'How?'

She shrugged. 'How would I know? I am trapped in these bloody cuffs.'

'Is there someone with you?' he asked.

She shook her head. 'I wish. All I know is someone will die. But there is a way to stop the killings.'

He narrowed his gaze. 'What?'

'Kill Asiloma. Your lieutenant and your...' she whispered, 'lover.'

For a moment Sheksh frowned. Outwardly, he wanted to laugh, but he was also frightened because the girl knew about him and Asiloma. 'Lover? Are you mad?'

'You can lie to me, but not to yourself.'

He wiped the sweat from his forehead. 'Kill him? And then the murders will stop.'

'Oh yes.'

'What kind of shit is this?' Seksh snorted a nervous laugh. He knew he wouldn't kill Asiloma. He simply couldn't. Not in a million years. 'You are bluffing, aren't you?'

There was a knock on the door.

Seksh saw Durga smiling as he walked to open it. There stood Asiloma, pale as ever.

'Someone killed one of our men,' he said.

At that, Seksh felt a cold tremor run though his entire body. He closed the door on Asiloma. Not saying a word, he grabbed hold of Durga shoved her against the wall, as hard as he could. 'How did you do it?'

She was in pain. The veins on her forehead had started to pop. But she was laughing. 'I didn't do anything. I was right here. How could I have done it?'

'No, you fucking did it! How did you do it? How?' he thundered, bringing the knife closer to her throat, but she was not afraid.

'Kill your lover or more will die,' her smile dissipated and there was darkness in her eyes.

'So this is your plan?'

'No.'

'Whose then? The Devas?'

'No.'

'Whose?' he screamed. He was pulling her hair, ripping strands right out of her scalp.

'Durga.'

He left her hair. 'What are you talking about? You say you are Durga but you say it's Durga's plan. What do you mean?'

'Oh no,' she chuckled, 'I just called you on the pretense that I'm Durga. My name is Katya, General Seksh. I *work* for Durga.'

14

Gauri was kept in a cage for a long time. She realised that she shouldn't have showed her face. Perhaps she could have instigated the attack on religion in some other covert way. She could have convinced someone else to do it.

But it was better than dying.

She knew the risks when she had joined Operation Nine Nights. She knew she could die and the plan would still move on. All that mattered was Mahisha's fall by the end of the ninth night.

It was perhaps the fourth day when the darkness finally gave way to light and she saw a sly, crony figure walking inside.

She could immediately recognise him. It was Shukr.

The lack of food and water had left her feeling weak and exhausted. Her body was frail and she was lying on the floor.

'How is your punishment going?'

'Kill me,' she replied. 'It'll be better.'

'Hmmm,' he contemplated, coming close to the cage. 'Why did you do it?'

She clenched her jaw, 'Because the rituals are wrong and wasteful.'

'Did I choose you for your morality, woman? I chose you because you listen to orders and execute them well.'

She remained quiet. She thought apologising could

work and get her out, but she hated Shukr's guts. He was a slimy man. And he was bad in his own way. She didn't want to touch his feet and do something she wouldn't be proud of.

'I know,' she whispered.

He knelt down, glaring at her. 'You have to realise who you work under is a god. And he has to be treated like that. Do not disrespect him.'

She was quiet yet again. She had one god, and it was not someone who wore buffalo horns.

'I feel keeping you here is doing a disservice to your skills. You are doing nothing but lying like a slugger. It's better that you serve your punishment and work at the same time,' he straightened. 'Your insubordination shall affect everyone. All two dozen of the women.'

She shot him a glare of contempt.

'Ah, angry are you? You should be. It's understandable. You care for your friends. They will face the brunt of what you've done, the same way you do.' He began to walk towards the door. 'You leave in an hour for the farm.'

The farm? She had not been to it for a long time. And she hated that place.

'You should feel lucky, girl, that I have not killed you,' he said. 'I should have...but I feel you can still redeem yourself.'

And he left. She stayed there, flaring her nostrils and yelling loudly. Screaming at the top of her voice till her throat became hoarse, she fell back on the floor and remained there.

Two dozen girls were put in a small caravan as it left for the farm.

They all were in a sullen mood, but Airavati's arms were around Gauri to comfort her. They had shawls wrapped around them for the weather had become chilly and the moon had begun to just peek over the sky. There were flaps at the end of the caravan, so they couldn't see where it was that they were going, but Gauri could see a bit. The streets were not made of granite anymore, neither were they marbled, but were dusty and barren. Pebbles and stones lay under the feet of strangers, and the picturesque hill forts of Mahishapur could be seen far in the distance behind them.

They were in the outskirts of the city.

'Don't you comfort her,' a woman chided Airavati. She was a grumpy, wrangly haired, and healthy woman who sat on the opposite side, and she had a double chin with two popping ears. The woman had a frown on her face and it struck Gauri that she had never seen her smile. Her name was Mata. 'It's because of her that we are here.'

'She was doing the right thing,' Airavati protested.

'There's no right thing in this world, girl. There are just different ideologies. One you think. One the other thinks. You differ. That's it,' Mata spewed her philosophical jargon. 'And now we are going to pull out the bloody corns and get flogged for doing our duty. Even if we do it well, we will get flogged. I tell you Gauri, if you pull this shit again, I will make sure I personally report you so at least we get saved. Right, girls?' And they all hurrayed.

Everyone hated the farms. The slaves would work along with the farmers who grew corn and other vegetables for daily wages. And they would constantly get flogged like animals for not being fast. People died either of exhaustion, heat, or just plain brutal beatings. The slaves had begun working here in the beginning and graduated to the palace where they were more respected. There were no cruel, callous floggers or torturers of any kind there.

'I am sorry,' Gauri meant it. Genuinely.

'Take your bloody sorry and shove it up your tiny ghost ass.' Mata growled and the rest of the girls laughed. She knew that Mata had a good following. She was called Mata because she was like a mother to other female slaves and convincing her meant convincing the entire group.

Gauri pursed her lips. She didn't care that there was so much of contempt towards her. But she had to speak out. 'I had to do it,' she blurted out, not caring about the consequences. 'What do you think we are? We are cattle for these men. We get hurt. We are in pain. We do what they want while they rule over us and we let it happen. We just keep letting it happen because we think we deserve it. But no. I say we don't. We don't deserve hatred and the system of oppression that we are subjected to. And so yes, that's exactly why I did what I did, and I will do it again if required. Because it's easy to stay quiet, but difficult to stay silent for me.'

They all looked at her for a moment. None of them showed any spark. Even Airavati. In fact, even Mata was quiet, but she was frowning yet again.

'I hope you all realise,' she concluded, 'we aren't slaves. We have to start fighting for what we believe in. For what we deserve.'

'And what is that?' Mata asked. 'Because I don't know what else there is except this.'

'The Aryas?' Airavati spoke up hopefully.

'They are as cruel as the empire we are living in.'

'No. Not the Aryas. Not the Dasas,' Gauri said. 'But a choice. A choice to be better.' She paused.

No one spoke. They remained silent. And so did Gauri. She was disappointed.

The whip came slinging across thin air as the man holding the torch smacked her in the back. Gauri felt a searing pain down her spine.

She fell down, but got up and began to work again. She couldn't say anything. Not a word. It was considered an act of rebellion if you did.

She was harvesting the corn and putting them in a storage wagon. She continued to do so. And got whipped again.

They were in the middle of a huge tract of land. The corn would be harvested, then get processed, peeled and exported to foreign lands.

She looked at the farmer who was beside her, doing the same thing. He had sunken bones and large scars on his back which he didn't pay heed to. This farm might have belonged to him, once upon a time. But not anymore. Everything was state-owned.

The guards would walk in their usual rotation with torches at night so they could see whether everyone was doing the job fast enough or not. No one was allowed to be asleep even if they had been in the field for a good few hours.

Gritting her teeth, Gauri continued to work. As much as she hated it, she simply kept her head down, her mouth shut, and worked. She glanced to her side to see Mata who was growling and getting whipped too. But not shooting her mouth off the way she was doing towards Gauri.

'What are you thinking, wench? Do your job well...' the guard brought the whip down sharply against her back...

And she grabbed it, twisting her hand instantly, holding on to the flogger's weapon with her red bruised arms. For a moment, he was stunned; he tried to pull it back but before he could do it Gauri recalled all her military training and pounced on him like a jungle cat.

Punching him straight in the nose and then stepping over his throat once he'd fallen over, she incapacitated the guard. The she began pummeling her fist into his mouth, breaking his teeth. She took the whip as another guard appeared on noticing the commotion, and she smacked it against the man's cheeks. He fell on the ground instantly.

Gauri looked at the farmer and at Mata, who were both taken aback by what she had done. And they didn't speak a word. Quiet. Shocked. Wide-eyed.

Then Gauri went to grab the fallen torch that had sparked a bit of a flame over the dried grass as she began to fan the fire in these crops. Slowly. The fire grew. Became crimson orange and then it rose, like the fire inside of her.

She turned back to Mata as the fire had caught up to her part of the crops too. And she could hear the commotion of the guards who were yelling now on seeing the growing flames, but they couldn't do anything.

She dropped the torch and sighed. She expected Mata to scream loudly that it was her. She did it. It was Gauri's fault.

But Mata said nothing.

Her silence was enough to make Gauri realise she was on the right path—to instigate rebellion along with her slave friends.

15

The king's court without the king was often an odd place. It was not a room. It was not even the palatial common halls where citizens would gather to see trials take place. No. It was in the bright open ground right outside the gates of the royal palace. A wooden pedestal was set up in the middle where the king or the subsidiary of the king would sit and execute justice. Here he was, right in the middle, Prime Minister Tamar whose job it was to execute justice now. In one sitting, he had to make multiple decisions. There were property disputes, murders, and other crimes.

And one of the cases was the rape case that Charini so excitedly sat for.

It was the fourth day of Nine Nights, and her plan till now was working as it should have, until she felt a tug in her heart and began to recall the conversation she had had with her estranged brother two days back.

She thought back to his revelation. A confession which had shaken her to the core. Bashkala was her brother. He had changed his name. He had become different. Quite different from what he used to be. But then it had been years since she had seen him. A man changes. A man stops being your brother.

She tried to concentrate on the crowd of people who were all either standing or sitting. They had all come for the trials, though in all honesty, they wanted to see the executions—pure, violent, sensational fun.

Charini sat in the front. Her eyes were on the Prime Minister. And he was worried. She could see it in his eyes. And if she could smile, she would. She was wearing her white clothes as usual, her face kept carefully blank. The plan was going well because now Tamar had to tell the world that the rapists would die.

And a revolt would begin.

And she would watch the show unfold.

But then, this was just one part of her elaborate scheme.

Memories resurfaced as she listened to Tamar address the other trials. She began to think about the conversation she had with Bashkala and how horrifyingly it had ended for her.

Two days earlier...

'Anna?' she could feel the words erupt with passion. And she felt something tug at her throat.

Bashkala was there. His face was impassive. 'Yes, it's me.'

'You are lying,' she knew he had the scar, and anyway, how would he know that she had a brother. She had not revealed it to anyone except the Devas. 'How did you know it was me?'

'Of course it's you. I am your older brother. I'd know my sister even though it's been more than a decade since I last saw you.'

'But...but you died.'

'Yes. I was horribly scarred. They took me to the infirmary. I worked as a slave. Rose up the ranks and became a captain,' he said, pursing his lips. 'And then I saw you. Getting close to Lady Sulochna. I took time to recognise you and then I saw the way you used your words, the way you spoke. I wasn't completely sure until I ransacked your room and found the pendant our mother had given you. And then I knew.'

He'd ransacked her room? She blinked, trying hard to gulp down what he had just told her.

'Why didn't you ever confront me about it till now, when you're accusing me?'

He had no response. But the lingering fear of rejection, she guessed. 'I don't know. I wish I could have. But something held me back. Something...' he shook his head. 'I can't explain.'

She didn't know whether she should hug him or not, but now she understood why Bashkala was always kind to her. It was because he wanted to be close to her. Like a brother.

'You are my sister and that is why I know for sure you have had a hand in this,' he said with renewed determination.

'If I did, would you turn me in?' she asked.

He couldn't respond. He was stunned for a moment. 'Did you? Or am I overthinking?'

She clenched her jaw. She had one burning question that had occupied her mind ever since his revelation.

'Why didn't you try to find me if you were alive?'

'Because...' he began, after a long, contemplative pause, 'I didn't want to find you.'

Charini saw the case that she had been waiting for had come before the court now.

It was happening.

The four rapists were called to the front, right below the pedestal, while the girl who was raped was called too, but she had a dupatta covering her face and she had come with her defeated parents. Charini saw Tamar, reading from the scroll:

'The events that I speak of are despicable and horrendous. It involves a complete negligence of the justice system and complete disrespect for the laws of the state.'

Charini saw the four men. They were chuckling. Not taking it seriously.

Even the men behind her murmured: 'They'll be fine.'

But Tamar spoke up high, 'Times are changing. We have shown growth as an empire. And we should show growth in our morals too. And for that reason, I hereby sentence the four perpetrators of this heinous crime to be sentenced to death.'

'Why?' she asked. She wanted to feel sad about it, this was the kind of behaviour she almost expected from him, for some twisted reason.

He lowered his gaze. 'I was a kid, Charini. A bloody child when everything I had was taken away from me.'

'I was raped, Anna. I was traumatized,' she said. 'I didn't want to take everything from you. But I was not your enemy.'

He was silenced by her sharp words. She had grit in her tone and she was furious at his stupid reasoning. But he continued:

'I thought I could get rid of you, so I went to the camp and purposefully got caught. I knew if I did that, I wouldn't live with the guilt of leaving you behind for some reason. And so, I did. And it went according to the plan. I didn't find you after that and was quite happy living a sombre life of a lonely man when I happened to see you again. It's like fate wanted us to be together,' he said. 'So I made sure you got close to Lady Sulochna and I tried to exercise my influence on the royal couple. They agreed to have you up close because of my words and now she's disappeared, and I feel guilty for trusting you.'

Charini didn't know what to do or say. So, it was him? It was a favour by him? She wasn't going to believe him. She knew she got the position through her shrewdness and her impeccable skills at being a companion to Lady Sulochna whenever she needed her.

'You know how people repress memories?' she asked casually.

He narrowed his gaze. 'What do you mean?'

'When you left me, a kind man helped me. Became my father, my brother. He helped me unlock a lot of my memories. He wanted me to figure myself out, to know why I had gone mute with my emotions,' she explained, revealing slices of the truth slowly. 'I remembered a lot of what I had purposefully forgotten. Things that had happened long ago.'

His face was growing pale.

'I remembered your conversation with the gramani when I was a child—something I had repressed.' She shook her head in disbelief even though she knew she heard it.

'What did you hear?' he asked, trying to be casual.

'That you, my dear brother,' she gave a plastic smile, 'were the one who had sold me to him, thinking what could an eight-year-old possibly do..What you hadn't considered was that I could *smash* his skull.'

At that, everyone rose. First there was pin drop silence. Then came the murmurs. Finally, people shouted. The four men watched in horror as they were pushed by the guards up to the pedestal where they were made to kneel down, four axemen making their way to them.

The revolt was strong. Voices and vulgarity were heard. People were trying to jump onto the pedestal but were pushed down by the soldiers. The ministers whose sons were up there were protesting but the Prime Minister didn't care.

He did what he had to do.

Charini saw the rape survivor. The girl had removed her dupatta and she was watching with relief and surprise at the turn of events.

The boys were crying. Weeping.

'We are young. We didn't know what we were doing.'

Of course you didn't know, Charini thought. After a long time, she felt herself smile.

The four boys were whimpering as the axemen came close, ready to do as they were told.

Charini wanted to see the violence. This was the first time she was enjoying it.

One by one, each axe swung.

The heads chopped off.

They fell on the ground with an ugly thud like disposable garbage.

One rolled close to the survivor's feet. She spat on it.

The men in the crowd began to shout in fear.

Fear that they were not exempt from committing any crime anymore. Fear that they finally would have to face the consequences of their actions.

Equality was a concept most men didn't understand.

And Charini, by doing this, just added a little spark to their understanding so it would burn like wildfire.

16

Today was the day she had begun to think she would never see.

Chandra stood up at the quarter deck from where the drums are beaten. There was a ledge on which she leaned while more than hundred people below her, looked up. They all wore similar looks of indignation. Of contempt. Everyone hated to be controlled and captained by a woman.

'I believe you all have received the news but I'm here to make it true and confirm it for you,' her voice rang loud and true. 'It is with great remorse that I inform you that the Admiral is dead.' Her eyes landed on the disbelieving Utharaka, who stood with his hands at the back, watching her with hawk eyes. 'A heart attack. He has left me in charge. I'm grateful that he thinks of me so highly. If anyone wants to dispute his decision, I have the written evidence to show you.' She had the unrolled scroll up and showed it to everyone. 'The Admiral himself has handed the duties to me,' she paused. 'I know many of you don't like me, but this is a team and I do not care whether you like it or not. These are the orders, and you just go with it. I want to believe that we can work as a team and respect the memory of the Admiral.'

The people were quiet. They all looked at her with a lethal gaze.

This was the time to reveal the plan.

'Our next mission is to go towards Ceylon.'

'And why is that?' one of them asked.

'Yeah, why Ceylon? We trespass in only the Sindhu Sagar. Nowhere else.'

'Because we need to be ambitious!' Chandra declared with a grin. 'And because I'm the captain and I can set course the way I want to.'

She could have had a mutiny on her hands but many of them respected the Admiral and believed in what he believed. They would take their time to warm up to her. But they would accept her soon enough.

It was the second day of the Nine Nights. She had to reach the borders of Ceylon in three days.

'Row! Row!' she cried. 'And let the blessings of Mahisha guide us!'

On the third day...

Utharaka entered the doctor's cabin where the body was displayed. The handsome face of the Admiral was right there. Pale.

His eyes were stark with sadness as he looked at his old boss and touched his cold skin. The doctor was on the side.

'What is it?'

'Heart, it seems like.'

'Any signs of poisoning?'

The doctor blinked in confusion. 'Poisoning, sir?'

'Yeah. Any red marks or any blisters or any bloody thing that points to poisoning?'

Utharaka knew that there was some foul play by the woman. She was a smart lass. She got up through the ranks in the ship quite fast and won over the Admiral too. She had her hair cut in the same way as the Admiral's wife. And he knew why. She wanted the Admiral to associate her with his wife. Who had died by the hands of the Devas. She was also quirky and smart and was apparently the captain now. Utharaka wanted enough proof to begin the mutiny so he could take her down and make himself the captain.

'Not really, no.'

'Strange.'

'Wouldn't it be strange if he were poisoned?'

'The reason I believe he is, doctor, is because such a fit man can't have a heart attack,' Utharaka rasped. 'He was poisoned and I don't know how you'll find it, but you have to. Think hard. Anything out of the ordinary?' He also had no external wounds, so poison had to be it.

'I can't be sure, I'll be honest. An in-depth autopsy has to be done and we are in the middle of the sea,' he paused. 'Though, there is something I noticed,'

He opened the corpse's mouth and pointed out the yellow layer over the tongue. 'He was close to vomiting. Not a usual sign in a heart attack. I found it strange. Plus, traces of wine in his system.'

Because he was poisoned. Utharaka grinned.

'So, the wine could be poisoned, yes?'

The doctor shrugged. It was far-fetched. But it could be true.

Utharaka walked to the cellar, still in deep thought about the entire thing. He was a young sailor when he had started off on a ship. It was a merchant vessel and he would sail from one place to another, delivering cargo to nearby islands or countries. That was about it. He had a family he fed. Soon, that family left him because he was not around much. The sea was what he loved the most and he continued to serve on it. They never understood his line of work despite his many attempts at explaining it to them. His children grew up without seeing him. His wife never talked to him. And he could now be a grandfather for all he knew, but it didn't matter anymore. To be part of a family, even his own, was a distant dream now.

So when a little mouse was trying to screw things up for everyone, he knew he had to make things right. He had to be better and prove to his estranged family that he was a good man doing good work.

The cellar had bottles. And he looked at the scrolls of where the wine bottle markings were written—how much had been consumed and how much was left. No one had drank since the Admiral's death, so he knew the last bottle that was pulled would be the one from which the Admiral had drunk. The bottle that killed him.

He had to find the bottle's name on the scroll so he could look into the garbage disposal and pull it out.

But there was nothing on the scroll. No mention that a drink was pulled out by the name of Chandra. He was disappointed.

He looked around the cellar, hoping to see an empty space, but all the bottles were where they were supposed to be. No one had pulled any out.

So the Admiral drank wine which was never pulled out? That meant someone had come in, taken the wine without letting the cellar in-charge know, and then kept it back. Since there were no labels, it was impossible to find the bottle amongst hundreds of them.

But there was one poisoned bottle here. And if he had to pull all of them out to find it...

'What are you doing here?' a voice was heard.

The boat rocked as he glared at the thin voice.

Chandra. She was standing there in her sherwani, looking like a boy under the fire lamp in the cellar. Her eyes were suspicious.

'Nothing to concern yourself with, captain.'

'I had a chat with the doctor,' she said, moving towards him.

'Yes?'

'He was quite curious about your theory,' she moved even closer. 'He asked if you were mentally stable. I promised him you are not. You are just mourning. Since it's absolutely far-fetched to think that someone poisoned the Admiral, right?'

He swallowed a lump. His eyes went down to the sabre Chandra was carrying; sheathed. And he had no weapon on him.

'It is indeed far-fetched, captain,' he tried to be respectable. Courteous.

She came closer.

If she can kill the Admiral, she can kill me.

'I believe you are right. But I think...' her hands came close to his forehead and she wiped off the beads of sweat forming there, 'I genuinely believe you have gone a wee bit mad after the demise of the dear old Admiral. I feel you must rest.'

'No, I am—'

'You are relieved of your quartermaster duties, Utharaka,' she smiled. 'You are ill. Get yourself checked.'

Two men came from behind. They were surely influenced by the little bitch, who took Utharaka by the arms.

'You can't do this to me!' he screamed, 'You can't!'

'Don't worry. I will drop you by the nearest island. You can check in at the infirmary and rest for the upcoming days. You are old and you do not belong on a ship anymore.'

The men were dragging Utharaka as he whimpered and cried, yelling: 'I know it was you, you little shit. I know it was you! YOU POISONED HIM!'

She didn't bother responding to his accusations.

'Lock him up. He is dangerous to not only the ship but himself.'

The men left with Utharaka. While he was gone, Chandra sighed in relief. She was *this* close to getting caught. She looked at the bottle. The poisoned one. It was right next to the shelf where Utharaka was standing. And it had a green stain on it, a leftover poison stain. And it smelt terrible if one brought it close to their nose.

Let's hope it's a smooth journey after this.

17

The clouds moved, and thunder danced in the skies elegantly, wavering like thin ribbons before vanishing.

Mahisha looked up, enjoying the sight. That was until his gaze fell on the Panas' celebrations. The Alani, a circle of priests and priestesses headed by Rigoli, were wearing synthetic masks of hounds and they had told the couples of the camp to band together and hold each other by the cheeks—to feel their presence. To attune themselves to nature. To especially Erdimpas, their virgin goddess. For the goddess accepted you not as a sole member, but with someone who was your soulmate. They did it every full moon, like today.

Mahisha glanced upon Thamisada who was kneeling in the corner with his men, the bright light of the burning fire glimmering against his iron helmet. The king of Maisuru was very interested in knowing what was under that helmet and why he hid behind it. But they weren't talking. Not for now. Alliances were all about negotiations and whoever spoke first would show desperation and would lead to the fall of the negotiation.

And Mahisha knew acting aloof was important right now.

He could see Thamisada didn't have his wife with him, and that made him curious.

'Will you join me?' he heard a voice.

Turning to the side, he saw the short-haired Tabita

with a grin like no one else's. She had a small face, diminutive compared to the largeness of Mahisha. He was a giant and she was a human. And she had the confidence that a giant possessed—her hands were splayed out in the front.

'Join you?' he was confused.

'Yes. In the ritual.'

Mahisha glanced at Trinetra who was as confused as him. But Mahisha knew that not joining could be considered as an insult to the tribe they were partnering with.

'Sure,' he came up on his feet, holding her hands.

She brought him close to the fire. Next to the dozen or so couples who were all touching each other's faces.

'I don't know what to do.'

'Well, what am I here for?' she smiled, bringing her hands close to his cheeks.

He pulled back. Fidgeted.

'What happened?' her smile faded.

'No...um...'

It felt like an intimate thing to do. Like her touching would be wrong. Was it his past getting in the way? But he took a deep breath and let her do it. She held his cheek in her hands. Her eyes glinted with excitement.

'You have to do the same,' she instructed.

And he did. His large palms crossed and laced across her olive skin, soft as satin.

'Now look into my eyes.'

'That's it?'

'It's easier said than done, your highness.'

He looked into her eyes. Deep. He tried to, at least, but he could only see her eyes. Her irises.

'Now forget about the world. Just belong to the moment, here, with me.'

'How does one do that?'

'Stop being afraid.'

'Afraid of what?' he asked indignantly.

'Accepting someone else in your life.'

'I don't want anyone else.'

'Are you sure?' she moved closer. 'Why did you become the ruler of Jambudvipa, your highness?'

He narrowed his gaze. He was losing concentration, but she had a firm grasp on his face, so he couldn't look away. It was right on her, and she was deeply acknowledging his presence.

'Because I wanted to be powerful.'

'That's it?'

He gritted his teeth.

'You wanted to be remembered?'

He nodded.

'You wanted to be acknowledged?'

He nodded.

'Are you lying right now?'

For some reason, the question made him teary. He swallowed back a lump in his throat as he took a deep breath. 'Yes, I am.'

'What is the reason you became the ruler, your highness?' she asked again, softly.

'Anger.'

'Towards?'

'The ones who ostracised my mother.'

She smiled. A delicate smile like a lotus flower. 'You hate your enemies because they threw her out like garbage?'

He nodded. 'I will throw them out of these lands the same way,' his eyes got teary.

'Why do I see guilt in your eyes then, my love?'

'Because...because I couldn't save her.'

'From?'

'My father.'

'So is it anger that drives you to rule these lands or the guilt that you couldn't do anything for your mother?'

He was confused. He was. He had no idea. He felt so many emotions running inside him. And now he was confronting them.

'Did she ever ask you to do this?'

'No. She never did.'

'What did she want you to be?'

His eyes widened. Tabita's face changed, evolving into his mother's, who had said to him: *'Be a good man, Mahisha. Be someone who everyone looks up to.'*

'But what if I can't? What if I turn out to be like father?'

'You won't. You can't. You have to be better than him.'

And he blinked. Tabita was there. His mother had left.

'She wanted me to be a good person,' he said hoarsely.

She smiled. 'And are you one?'

He shook his head. 'I am not. I am the worst man to be born on this world.' And he began to cry, but he didn't bow or move. His eyes were drawn to her.

'Who was your father?' she asked.

'An Arya. And she was a Dasa. They had fallen in love. And they were ostracised for they were inter-caste. My father hated that fact and blamed it on my mother, said it was her fault.'

'Does your hatred towards the Aryas stem from your father?'

He nodded. He hadn't thought about it. He always thought about Aryas as vicious, drunkard rulers, but now he realised it was far more complicated than that. It was always about his parents. And about how he had internalised it. He was part Arya and part Dasa. He always had been. But he used to ignore this part about his life and not tell anyone. Not disclose that his mother wasn't the only one who was ostracised but his father too.

'You have conquered more than you ever could and now...it's time for you to change, perhaps?'

He nodded. 'I suppose it is.'

And then she removed her hand from his cheek. And went for a hug. He was frozen for a moment, realising he had confessed so much for some reason. A melancholic tune played in the background, and the sound of tambourines permeated the air. He held her back too and he smiled. She was trying to bring the best out in him.

Something his mother used to do, before she died.

'I don't understand why I became like my father,' he said to himself, whispering.

And he had no answer for it. Perhaps he associated himself with his father. Perhaps he realised he couldn't be better than him.

And his eyes drew towards Thamisada who was watching them from afar.

Mahisha knew what he had to do now.

They walked to the outskirts of the camp where the thorn-like barricades were put up. Sharp spikes intermingled to keep others out. Booby traps were placed outside those, while scouts were stationed on trees so they could watch out for any incoming attacks. Within the camp, there was dance and music.

Thamisada had his goat milk in a mug, while Mahisha refrained from drinking any milk and was holding his wine.

'I suppose Tabita and you are getting closer,' he said with a chuckle.

'She can be quite convincing,' Mahisha smiled.

'When she wants something, she gets it.'

'Where's your wife?'

Thamisada was taken aback. 'She's passed.'

'I see. I apologise.'

'No. No. She died quite early in Tabita's life.'

Mahisha was surprised Thamisada didn't marry anyone else, since he didn't have a woman around him. 'Why don't you ever take your helmet off?'

He sighed, 'It's a strange habit, I suppose.'

'Habit?'

'I was young when I was caught in a fire. Our camp was raided, and you see, I was one of the victims. Surviving victim. I was wholly burnt, and from then on, I have worn the helmet. It makes me feel...'

'Less insecure about your skin?' Mahisha knew that feeling because he himself had blotches of green skin and he hated it. He was a premature baby and it had resulted in discolouration of skin.

'Yes, indeed. But I am glad you don't carry that insecurity with you.'

He would have gotten angry in any other scenario, but it was not the case anymore. He was only angry at his skin because he was shamed for it, but he had realised the one who had shamed him was prejudiced against him, as she was a spy of the Devas. It had nothing to do with him, and he had begun to accept that.

'I have to tell you something,' Mahisha finally sighed in confession. 'We can go back and forth on this. Stay quiet. But unfortunately, there's no point. I need you, Chief Thamisada, on my side, and I have begun to believe that perhaps I have to not be so stubborn with my thoughts. I believe it's time for me to settle down.'

Thamisada chuckled and his voice came heavy. 'You are accepting the marriage?'

'Yes, I am,' he couldn't believe he was saying it.

Thamisada came forward and put his hands on Mahisha's shoulders. 'Well, I suppose everything will now go just as we had planned.'

Trinetra was worried about Mahisha. He could feel something was not right. And here he was, lying next to the wench in his tent, drinking wine from his goblet. He had to find out what was going on here. Rigoli had learnt that Durga was here, but she was nowhere to be found. He had sent his men and none of them seemed suspicious except one who had come to him and told him something:

'There's something strange about these people. I have met Scythians and they don't behave like the ordinary Scythians.'

But Trinetra didn't consider it as a big issue for Scythians had hundreds of tribes and the Panas were just one of them. His soldier was just overreacting. Overthinking.

And then the other news popped up from one of his scouts. A band of Devas were seen in the outskirts of Kanchipuram. They had disappeared, but their last location could be tracked easily. He wanted to explore that; he would talk to Mahisha about it...

A shadow entered the tent. The wench was sleeping on his side. The diya cast a light, and the unmistakable glint of a blade could be seen.

Trinetra realised the blade was moving towards him and it slashed him in the stomach. Gutted him out as another hand wrapped around his mouth to silence him. He couldn't move for long, his eyes rolling back, but he managed to catch a glimpse of the killer.

'It's...you...' he whispered.

He knew the killer.

But before he could scream it out...

He was dead.

18

Seksh couldn't help but remember the incident.

The incident that made him sure he was not human. He had a violent streak. He had come to the house of the couple. And he had killed one of them while the woman had escaped. The boy had begged him to leave her.

But Seksh hadn't. He had chopped the boy's head off. And then moved for the door. Bursting through it, he realised the woman had managed to escape through the window. Seksh, with his blade in hand, prowled to the window and his eyes darted over the shadows of the woods. There was none he could see.

The woman had disappeared. Gritting his teeth, he stamped his foot.

When Mahisha demanded a girl, you had to get her for him. Otherwise, he could get pretty angry. She was a young potter. Barely fifteen. But Mahisha didn't care about age. She looked older than she was.

Unfortunately, Seksh hadn't seen much of her other than the fact that she had big, thick curls that covered most of her face.

For some reason, the image of those curls and that day brought a lot of nightmarish visions in front of Seksh. He himself had tried decoding it, but he couldn't.

Asiloma was standing in front of him. In the captain's lodge. The silver light of the moon had filtered inside the room.

'So you don't know who killed the man?'

Asiloma shook his head. 'She wants me to die?'

Seksh had told him about it. He couldn't hide such an important fact. He saw him and felt sad. Asiloma was the most important man in his life, but he also couldn't risk people like this. Seksh could feel the burden on his chest. The guilt that was slowly suffocating him. 'We will figure something out,' he said with more confidence than he felt.

'I think this Durga woman is amongst us.'

'Could be,' Seksh sighed, trying to distract himself. 'Let's have dinner. I told the cook to make your favourite.'

The feast on the table in the common halls of the outpost—where the chill was more and warmth from the hearth was less—had nice chicken legs with the skin peeled off, served with broccoli, corns and potatoes. Only Asiloma and Seksh were at the table, while his favourite cook was serving them.

'Good job,' he told the cook.

She offered a weak smile. 'Thank you, general,' she said as she left.

'Don't you get scared of that bald head?' Asiloma leaned forward. 'She's so creepy, with no hair,' he paused. 'Do you know why it is like that?'

Seksh shook his head. He never cared to ask and now he felt guilty for that too. He was feeling guilty about doing little things the wrong way.

As he feasted on the chicken leg, he saw Asiloma and couldn't help but feel safe in his presence. He had met the man when he was on one of his military campaigns and he was about to get married to one of his allies. Mahisha had organised the alliance, but Seksh couldn't go through with it. He lied through his teeth that he couldn't consider marrying women, that he just liked to have fun with them, and Mahisha had patted him on the back for it.

Later, he was visited by Asiloma who remarked how he had seen Seksh staring at him in the camps outside while he was bare-chested. Seksh had gotten offended and slapped Asiloma. And then he kissed him. Because he had really wanted to. He found Asiloma to be exceptionally attractive. It was supposed to be a one-night fling but now it had become an entirely different thing.

After eating the food, he called the cook again and handed her the letter to deposit to the messenger. He had kept the letter on the side the entire time, contemplating over it, whether to send it or not. The cook nodded and did so.

'What does the letter contain?'

'It's to be sent to Kanchipuram. To Mahisha.'

'And why is that?'

'To come here when he's done forming the alliance. I would like him to meet the Durga.'

Asiloma shook his head. 'But she's not Durga.'

'I don't believe her.'

'Great then. We have to wait here now till he comes.'

'Just a matter of few days.'

There was a brief moment of silence between them.

'Why would she...' Asiloma leaned forward, whispering, breaking the awkward silence. 'Could it be supernatural?'

'What do you mean?'

'Could there be a spirit called Durga?'

Seksh wanted to almost laugh. 'Do you hear yourself?'

Asiloma was offended and pulled back. 'How could this woman know that someone would die when there is no one besides us here?'

'Because she has someone hiding right now. Gather your men and search every bloody corner. I know there's the real Durga hiding here, somewhere.'

Asiloma nodded.

But he would be lying if he didn't admit that he was afraid right now. He definitely was.

What better way, he thought, of fighting fear than by confronting it?

'CHUDAIL! DAKA! CHUDAIL! DAKA!'

She heard the echoes in her ears. She was small. She was running. There was sand. All over the place. Like a desert. There were mountains and heaps of sand. And there she was. She had a young face. A cute one. She had beautiful emerald eyes. Her mouth had broken milk teeth, and strands of loose hair fell over her face. The wind was hot and so was her feet, which sunk into the sand.

People were running after her. And her mother. They were being chased. There were spears and blades in their hands. Aimed at them.

'CHUDAIL!' someone shouted. She could feel the words piercing her soul.

They thought they were witches. Rumours were spread when Mahisha's men were almost exposed by them in a small town. Katya and her mother had seen them stealing some important cargo that was supposed to go to the town. But they were going inside Mahisha's coves. They were caught by Mahisha's men, but they escaped. They had intended to tell the gramani, but the gramani was easily influenced by the men first. They said the two women were chudails. They were witches. They practiced black magic.

And soon, the whole village was after them.

Nobility was wrong.

Katya opened her eyes watching the iron grilled prison bars in front of her.

Nobility was wrong.

She repeated under her breath. Nobility was for people who were idealists. But the ones who survived were the ones who were shrewd and pragmatic and smart. Real smart. You couldn't just be good. You also had to think two steps ahead. You had to play mind games. You had to manipulate.

Unfortunately, you had to do all of this because if you didn't, you'd be the odd one out.

The prison doors opened, and she saw Seksh enter.

He was a good-looking man barring the eye that had a long scar on it, making him look scarier than a regular man.

'I thought I would sleep alone tonight. Care to join?' she pointed to the granite floor with a straight, plastic smile.

He stood there in silence. His brows arched. She could see that he didn't know why he was standing here. He just wanted to see her. Know that she was human and not something else.

'How long do you plan to continue this?'

'What?' she asked.

'Kill my men one by one.'

'One by one? Oh, that's not it.'

'What do you mean?'

'Oh, um...so since you ignored my request, it's going to be worse now,' she smiled.

'What do you mean?'

She chuckled.

'Durga doesn't take it lightly when people don't listen to her. And you didn't listen to her, so now...' she looked out. They would be coming anytime soon. 'You will have a massacre on your hands.'

'Is this some kind of a joke?'

'Am I laughing?' she asked, her face placid.

'When?' he asked.

'Oh.' The clouds moved. The moon was visible. 'Now.'

And then they both heard the hoots and the cries. There were Seksh's men shouting outside. Loudly. The doors were being banged open and everything could be heard. The zapping of arrows and clanging of blades.

'What have you done?' Seksh asked but didn't

wait for a response, locking the prison door and rushing out.

As he came out of the building which had all the prison cells, he saw his men sprawled on the ground.

He pulled out his weapon, when he finally noticed what the rest of his men were fighting against...

They all had long, wiry hair tied in ponytails and were wearing nothing but loin cloths. They were all heavily scarred. With weapons in their hands, they were ruthless. Like feral animals.

One of them reached close to Seksh who defended himself by deflecting the spear. But the feral man still prowled towards him, and so Seksh moved aside and pierced the blade in the man's back. He fell down yelping.

Seksh's archers were shooting arrows—some aimless, some hitting the target, but they were all over the place.

In all the mayhem, he was searching for Asiloma, who was in the corner and was fighting with his long spear as well. But, when the feral man came towards him—

He simply passed Asiloma. Not attacking him.

As if...

As if...

They were instructed to not hurt Asiloma in any way.

A man came from the back, slamming Seksh to the ground. He turned around to see a feral man with a thick beard, right before he punched Seksh in the face—

his jaw faced the brunt of it and he spat blood. While he tried to get the man off him, an arrow pierced his head and he flung back.

Seksh came on his feet and saw another feral man moving for him. In a flash, he swung his blade in the air, cutting through the wind and smacking the man on the head. He fell on the ground instantly.

He noticed the rest of the feral people began to disperse. As quick as possible. Scurrying like rats.

'FOLLOW THEM AND KILL EACH ONE OF THEM!' Seksh screamed.

And his men nodded. With the horses still there, his men left the outpost to search for these people. Seksh limped over to Asiloma, hugged him and asked: 'Are you fine?'

'They didn't attack me,' he was shocked. 'I killed a few but they didn't even defend themselves.'

'Because she wants *me* to kill you. She won't have it any other way,' Seksh kicked the ground with his unhurt leg. 'She's playing games with us. Why couldn't we see the attack coming?'

'It was dark and we were getting lazy,' Asiloma cursed under his breath. He knew he was wrong here, giving such a flimsy excuse.

Seksh saw the men around. Almost forty of his men were dead in this slaughter. Just because he didn't listen to Katya. Now, even if they wanted to leave the outpost, they couldn't. They had to wait for a rescue party to come and gather around, for Seksh didn't know how many more surprises Katya held.

'Were they...'

'Bandits, yeah. Looked like it. Forest bandits. Nishadhs,' Asiloma specified the native term that was used for them. Nishadhs stayed in the trees and used the grass or the bushes as their camouflage. They were feral people, but they were also good at taking orders. There was one amongst them who would be learned and knows how to communicate. They could be easily bought by an outsider.

Which is what Katya must have done. She must have paid them as a separate army to attack at a specific time like tonight.

'Arghh...'

Seksh heard the sound. He began to stagger towards it and saw a nishadh groaning, a deep wound on his arm. Seksh knelt and brought him closer to his face, grabbing his throat. 'Who sent you?'

'She's coming...she's coming... She will kill all of you...' the man maniacally laughed and his pupils dilated.

He looked at Asiloma.

He was worried.

Mahisha was going to come once he received the message and if he saw all this was happening, he would question Seksh why he hadn't done what he was asked to do. After all, for Mahisha, Asiloma was just another soldier in his army.

And Seksh almost regretted sending the messenger.

19

Gauri was thankfully saved after that day of mayhem.

And it was the fifth day of Nine Nights and things were probably going on smoothly at her end, though she didn't know. She had yet to figure out exactly how to stir more problem. But Mata was on her side. She wasn't sure. She hadn't tattled to the guards even when they asked who was responsible for the farm fires. Due to the flames, it had led to a large number of farmers being relieved from their duties for the time being, and had resulted in a huge loss for the empire as their main production had been hampered.

Gauri was calmly sitting down in her room, mulling over other ideas of what else she could do, when she saw the door in front open and found Airavati with a young, shabby-haired boy beside her. For a moment, she was surprised to see the young boy. He had a wooden figure in his hand, with which he was busy playing, and dirty stains marked his fat cheeks.

He was cute and reminded her of the young boys she used to thieve around with, but maybe he wasn't so devious.

'Who is he?' she asked.

'Om,' she replied, but the boy didn't care. 'Guru Shukr wants me to keep a look over him while he handles a few things. I was told to stay in the common room, but I sneaked out. He's calling a meeting of all the ministers in the catacombs of the palace.'

That was strange.

Gauri walked to Om and touched his face. Looked at him. He seemed dazed. 'Was he offered anything to drink?'

'He was drinking ordinary milk by the time I got him. And Shukr also said that I have to stay clear from you since you are a troublemaker. So my obvious course of action was to bring the boy to you, defying him,' she grinned.

Airavati was undeniably on her side and Gauri had convinced her to alert her of anything fishy.

Like this.

'I think he's drugged,' she looked at the boy's eyes again. 'He's slipped into this daydream sort of a trance.'

She had heard about it. She had, in fact, studied it. She remembered:

Yama kept the stack of scrolls in front of her, while he pulled up a chart and made her read it. In the middle, there were a few diagrams. One of them was a boy's image, who was being put into a hot boiling cauldron while men with hoods were circled around.

'When you'll infiltrate the palace of the subject,' Yama began talking to his fifteen-year-old apprentice, 'remember one thing: you are going to witness dark things.'

'Like?'

He signalled to the diagram. 'It's called Nanban. Child sacrifices.'

'Child...' she widened her gaze. 'Are you joking?'

The bald man's face was tight and unnerving. 'What do you think?'

'But that's...'

'I know. It's a concept they have stolen from the Egyptians. Apparently they believe that if a virgin boy or a girl is sacrificed, they shall bring riches, honour, and glory to the ruling king. Shukr is the originator of that. And this is the most vicious crime you can commit.'

'So does everyone know of this?'

'Only the elite people. Not even slaves or guards are allowed. They know that sometimes a child comes but never leaves.'

She looked at the boy again. Glaring at him with precision. 'He's going to be sacrificed.'

For a moment, Airavati was in complete disarray. Frozen. And then she mumbled, 'Are you...wait...what?'

'Yeah.'

'Um...why?'

She didn't want to go through the explicit explanations right now. She knew she had to save the boy.

'How many guards in this corridor?' she asked.

'Quite a few. As always, they are doing rotations.'

She began to plan. She had to figure out a way to save the boy. But...she looked at her cot and then at the boy again. He was drowsy. Couldn't speak much. And was also quite thin.

She took him by the arm and put him on her cot, placing a blanket over him so his entire form was covered.

'What are you doing?' Airavati asked.

'Taking him out.'

'But Shukr left him with me...'

'Tell him he ran or lie. Figure out something. You are smart,' Gauri said, as she dragged the mattress and took it outside with the boy on it.

Airavati stood there, too confused to speak.

But Gauri didn't care. She knew that Airavati was quick enough to think of a lie or even tell the truth if that'd buy more time. Now she had to take the child back to his parents.

Returning...

She had dragged the cot towards the gate of the back alley of the palace where a guard was standing. As he looked up, he raised his brows.

'What are you doing with that mattress?'

'Rats!' she screamed, and he immediately got scared.

'Oh!'

And he saw something moving in the sheets. 'But there's something...'

She gulped nervously. 'Yeah, because there are still rats. I have to dispose it off on the street. Let me go!'

'I'll help you...'

'NO!' she screamed again and then composed herself. 'You must understand, sir, that I can let myself be harmed, but I will not let you be harmed. You are an important ally to the crown. Look at you—so smart, so intelligent.'

He was getting happy about having his praises sung.

And she left his gaze, dragging the mattress out in the open and pulling it towards the streets.

Shukr had ordered his men to bring Airavati to him while he waited in his office. He shouldn't have given the boy to that woman, or to any slave in fact. But he had no choice. She was the one at hand when there was an emergency with the cauldrons. His men had got the wrong size and he had had to go downstairs and check himself before coming up and waiting for that slave.

His men allowed Airavati to enter the halls. He found her without the boy.

Without the...

'Where's the boy?' he asked sharply.

'Uh, he ran,' she was frightened. Mumbling out of fear.

'He ran?' He couldn't have. He was drugged. 'Tell me the truth, girl.'

He could see she was going white and ordinarily he would have tortured her, but he just held his gaze directly at her. He didn't have time. 'Tell me, where is he?'

She didn't respond. He grunted. Quick torture time, perhaps, he thought.

She was pushed on the ground by the guard behind her and a knife was put against her throat.

'Tell me, or you'll die. Your life is not that important to me, girl.'

Airavati contemplated for a moment and then nodded hesitatingly.

By the time, she had escaped the palace and was in the midst of the streets where the sun was beating down, she lifted the sheets and pulled the boy up, making him stand properly, though he was all wobbly, but still clutching on to his doll.

'Where's your house, kid?' she asked urgently.

And she heard it. The loud hoots were audible. Men were scurrying through the streets.

Airavati must have been forced to give out the truth. She bit her lips.

'I suppose we have to run. Can you manage it?' she asked him.

'Murmur...lion...rawr?' he said.

'Seems appropriate for this scenario, I suppose,' she picked him up thanks to all the strength she'd built during her training sessions where she was made to lift heavy things and do a lot of exercises. She was trained by military veterans.

She began to run towards the alleys and the lanes, moving as far away as she could from the men, who were moving through the streets on horsebacks now, while some were asking around about the girl with a child.

'Home...street...' the boy in her arms smiled absently.

'Is it on this side?' she was hopeful.

He was just grinning. She could see his fingers were

pointing out to something. She began to walk in that direction, as suspicious eyes began to follow her. She was coming close to the depression in the middle of the city, a downward slope which ultimately took one to the shacks and the poor homes.

She began to descend towards it.

And heard hooves.

They were moving for her.

She turned back. There was a horseman with a sword in his hand.

Oh, by the heavens...

She instantly dodged the sword, crouching as it swung for her and found that the horse had moved in front of her now. It turned and began to gallop towards her...

She slammed against the face of the horse with the help of a fallen shield, as the animal and the man on it crashed on the ground.

Then she began to run faster, sprinting. She was already struggling because she was carrying a boy in her arms.

'Home...' he said, 'oh wee oh wee...'

She had moved to the line of shacks, and she kept asking the boy which one was his, but the boy wasn't acknowledging any so she knew they weren't his home. She passed the street when a smooth cut of a lane arrived and she found a guard springing up with the blade. She used the boy's legs to smack him in the face, and she must have struck hard enough for he fell to the ground.

'Oh wee wee...' the boy was clapping excitedly. 'Home...'

She saw where he was pointing. With drool dribbling down his face and his droopy eyes, he was still able to point out the shack that belonged to him. She walked to it, passing through the flap in the front, and inside she found a couple. They were both sitting on the ground, when they saw Gauri place the boy down.

'What are you doing?' they asked in shock. 'Oh! It's him! Oh my baby boy!'

She smiled. She had reunited the family.

'Where did you find him?' the man asked with worry.

'Don't speak.'

She heard the numerous footsteps in the back. The guards had surrounded the shack. She instantly went to the corner to hide herself and told the parents to shush up while she was here. The guards moved around, scanning the place.

She remained still. She knew that her cover as a slave has been blown and she couldn't go back there. She had to find a way to disrupt the religion of the state from the outside now...

'SHE'S HERE!' the man whose son she just saved shouted to the guards.

'No, no...what are you doing?'

The guards came in, viciously grinning at the sight of Gauri as they caught hold of her and shoved her to the ground.

'We had no hand in it. We don't even know her,' the man said. 'The child is still yours.'

And the mother kissed her boy before she handed the sheepish, drugged child back to the guards.

'No...NO!' she screamed, but her hands were pulled

back behind her and she was being pushed outside, so she could be sent to prison for good. 'Why did you do it? He's your son. He's your bloody son!'

As she was whisked away, the parents replied, and she heard their final words: 'The God Mahisha will be proud of our sacrifice and shall bestow us with riches and more children in the future. We cannot anger our god.'

Then she was dragged to the chariot, on which she was put while guards surrounded her, driving her back. She didn't protest any longer, for she knew that the real enemy weren't these little putrid sacrifices, rituals, and the orthodox system. It was...

Her eyes gazed at the golden statue of Mahisha. Fifty feet tall. It was a temple which didn't belong to the women. Men could come and ask for their battles to be won, both internal and external. The statue was considered so imbued with supernatural powers that wishes were apparently granted and no one would even break rules around it. It was sacrosanct.

And she knew that to remove the idea of Mahisha as a god from people's minds, she has to *show* them that Mahisha was no god.

20

Bashkala was playing chaturanga with a fellow soldier in a small gambling den that was stationed in the upper part of Mahishapur. People came here to play games or to bet on chariot races. They would drink and get wasted. Here, one could get specialised betel leaves with a hint of the illegal Soma in it, to get a high. Bashkala, being a captain himself, knew he could bust the den, but then where would he play his games? Get rid of his angst and his worries that plagued him and made him guilty?

The Govinkartana, who was the gamekeeper, announced the winner of the game—Bashkala. He grinned, feeling smug, while the person looked disheartened.

He was a bad man. He knew. He had done a lot of things for money. Especially selling off his sister. He always had money on his mind. It was the bloodthirsty greed.

'Concentrate more, Shiva,' he grinned as he took the mug and threw the remnants of the wine back in his greasy mouth, spilling half the contents over his thick, charcoal beard.

A man came beside him. Sitting next to him, he handed Bashkala a small parchment.

'Captain, received some intelligence.'

He looked at the man. He was no soldier. He was a ragpicker, by the looks of it.

'Who the fuck are you?'

'One of your men was asking some questions and was giving some good chicken in return for some information on the Prime Minister's wife's whereabouts.'

He raised his brows. The wine had made him slightly sluggish. 'Was he now?' He didn't know his men were doing such things. 'Where is she?'

The man nudged the paper. 'Written here.'

He read it. It was in the outskirts of the city. A barren land that he knew of. With heaps of sand around, and roads that led to nowhere.

'Are you sure?'

'Few people have seen her there.'

'Why was she there?'

He shrugged, 'Beats me. Just know she was last seen there.'

'Do you know boy, you are the tenth person who has come to me with her last probable location?' He burped, getting angry. But since it was his job, he had to check the location out and see if there was actually anything there or not. It had almost become a chore, so he had stopped taking it seriously and looked at it more as a mere formality.

'Ugh,' he took his sheathed silver sword and wore it on the girdle around his waist, then rolled up the parchment and tossed it in the corner. 'Thank you.'

And the man left. The captain manoeuvred out, gathering his coins from the winnings he had made in the den. Burping his way out of there, he found that a horse and his backup men who accompanied him everywhere were waiting for him.

'Come on,' he ordered sluggishly as the bright, silver light of the moon shone over them, 'we have a lead.'

Tamar was getting extraordinarily worried. Men had gathered around his house and were protesting. The women, this time, weren't making much of a fuss. At least, he had that to be glad about. No one was happy with the decision, and the ministers' whose sons had died, had already written to Mahisha about the goings on at the court. They had decided to take him down by reporting him to Mahisha.

But Tamar was afraid for Sulochna. It had been two days since he had executed his judgement and there was still no news from the kidnapper.

It wasn't until the evening, when the moon had risen, that he was told by one of his soldiers that a letter was found outside the village which had the location of his wife.

Gathering up his men, he moved for the doors and was out on the streets in no time. He knew moving across the bunch of men who were at the gate would be tough, so they took the back gate, which led to narrower streets.

'You should wear this,' his guard said, holding a hooded cloak in his hand.

Tamar nodded, wearing the desired camouflage. He thought of taking Charini with him, but then she was just a handmaid and nothing else. Just a doctor to Sulochna and she could visit Sulochna and check up on her when he got her back.

If he got her back.

Bashkala was closing in on the outskirts of the village with his horses and men. Today, he was moving slower than he was supposed to. He looked at the two men, beside him who were constantly making sure their captain wouldn't doze off.

At night, the sands were calm. Spirits existed here, he had heard. It was a bright, hot, sunny desert outside Mahishapur which stretched up to the hills and then moved for the ravines and the civilisation. But it wasn't bright at this hour. Nor hot. Oh no, it was chilly. The moonlight glinted eerily over it. Wind was whipping across his face, as he finally reached the place he was supposed to.

It was right up against the hills, near a rocky scaffold where enemies would sometimes take refuge. Since it was the outskirts, the spies or enemy squads often lurked here. But since there was no one opposing them, it was empty now.

'We are done. Let's go back,' he said in a bored voice, and they turned their horses without any protest. Just then, they heard something like a mewl.

A cry.

Of a woman.

Even in his drunken stupor, Bashkala could vouch

for the fact that it sounded like Lady Sulochna. He dismounted his horse along with his guards, and moved forward, searching the rocks to finally find a woman. She was lying under a blanket of night and groaning in pain.

'Lady Sulochna...' all his sluggishness was slowly leaving him as he inched towards the person. 'Lady Sulochna...'

And he turned her over so he could see her face.

As soon as he did, he turned pale with shock.

Tamar reached the location and as much as he hated it there, that was it—a temple house that was first started by Shukr. It was empty, isolated as it was, close to the western watchtower. It acted as a ghost temple for people to come, but in reality it was in this state because Shukr was now busy concentrating on the bigger ones. It was supposed to be taken down, but Shukr insisted that a temple should not be destroyed even if the statue of Mahisha it contains in it is a small figurine.

Tamar knew very well that Shukr's religious spiels were bullshit. It was to earn money, fool people, and keep them in fear. Shukr had admitted to as much, long back: 'Faith is the greatest weapon you can use against people without even touching them.'

Tamar had a hard time believing it, but when he saw the results, he was surprised. Shukr had some foresight.

The old ghost temple was important for another reason too. This was the one from where it had all started. Tamar was the last one to come to the temple, a woodcutter's son. Shukr saw the fire in him when the Devas had ransacked Tamar's house. Shukr took him on board. The temple was where they all had trained and learnt from their guru.

And now it lay covered in cobwebs.

It showed how their ego and their attitude had made them forget where they had come from. But when Tamar, with his soldiers, walked inside the temple, he felt a strange sort of warmth arise from an otherwise cold place.

'You should stay inside. Let us first secure the perimeter,' his guard suggested, to which Tamar just glared.

It was his wife. He wanted to find her himself first.

He walked in. And he saw there was a woman clad in all white. Alone. Wrapped in ropes. Unable to move. His soldiers searched every room of the temple as Tamar reached the woman, knelt down, and began to untie her. When he was done, he took the ball of woollen cloth out of her mouth which had so far stopped her from screaming.

And then the woman hugged him. Sulochna was grasping him tightly. And they embraced for a while in silence with not a word spoken between them, as Tamar felt elation zinging through him. He was able to rescue her. She was here and he thanked the gods, even if he wasn't sure they existed.

'I have to tell you something,' she said. 'Something very, very important.'

It was Charini.

She was on the ground and she had a dagger in her hand with which she instantly stabbed Bashkala in the chest. For a moment, Bashkala was frozen, confused. He wanted to remove it, to pull the dagger out, but before he could, he fell to the ground. The two guards who were with him pulled out their weapons and moved for Charini.

She was not good with weapons. But she was angry. And she hadn't expected Bashkala to be part of this mission. If there was someone to kill, it was him. And she would do it with her own hands, without shrewd manipulation.

As Bashkala was trying to take control and trying to pull the dagger out, Charini quickly stole his sword, unsheathing it and rolling out of the vicinity of the two soldiers who had come to attack her.

She stabbed one of them in the back, while she kicked the other one to the ground. The one on the ground grabbed her by the feet and pushed her onto the floor.

The surviving guard began to scramble across the sandy floor, trying to reach her, to choke her, when she took a handful of sand and just threw it vengefully at the man's face and he went blind for a moment. She punched his head, and as he fell down, she climbed on top of him, grabbing the rock next to him...

And slamming it on his head. Hard.

Taking a deep breath, it dawned on her that she had just killed someone, she moved to the side and began to regain control of herself. Murder...murder... she had not done enough ever.

It was the plan. Send two letters. One to Tamar with the correct location. Another to Bashkala with the incorrect one. First send fake messages to Bashkala with fake locations that Sulochna was there, so he would stop taking it seriously and then provide him with this location finally, on the night he's drunk and not careful. She had to be patient and had to plan perfectly, sync with Bashkala's gambling routine, for the execution to take place.

She was expecting no guards, but Bashkala had brought them.

She began to limp over to Bashkala, who was still trying to pull the dagger out, but it had penetrated his lungs and blood was dripping from his mouth. He was weak. He looked half dead, as she pushed the dagger deeper into his flesh with her foot.

He whispered: 'I'm your brother…' the light almost leaving his eyes.

'No, you are a fucking pimp.'

'I have to tell you something.'

She looked tired. There were puffy eye bags under her eyes. She was dishevelled too, her hair all over the place.

'What is it? Do you know who kidnapped you? Did you see that person's face?'

'I did, yeah. And you won't believe it,' she said.

'Who? Who is it?'

She swallowed a nervous lump and said: 'Shukr.'

21

She was *this* close to reaching the goal.

She was where she was supposed to be and according to her count—it was the fifth day. And now at any moment, there would be a big ship that she would have to deal with.

The days preceding this had gone smoothly, especially since they had dropped off the crazy Utharaka on an island. No one in the beginning believed that he was mad, but he was spouting some really stupid stuff, leading the ones who were under him to doubt his superstitions. Worse, his reputation was something not everyone liked. He was a bossy man and people hated him and his hawk nose which he was always poking into people's business. On the other hand, Chandra was a nice person. Likeable. Kind to all her sailors. And they took to a kind person over a flimsy man.

She was at the quarterdeck waiting for the action to begin, her spyglass hanging from her neck, when she looked up and saw the ship from afar. It was right there, sailing towards Jambudvipa.

'What are we attacking, captain?' one of the sailors who was standing below asked her.

'A ship that the Admiral wanted to attack,' she lied. 'He left me a letter saying so.'

'All righty, move on then,' the sailor ordered

the oarsmen who were all rowing in the direction of the ship.

Reaching a hundred yards of the enemy ship, she knew the battle would be against formidable foes. Two ships were never within hundred yards of each other unless there was a battle at hand. And so, without hesitance she ordered her men to get the artillery ready. The oarsmen were told to wear all the armour to protect themselves while soldiers with shields were directed to protect the oarsmen, since they were the drivers of the ship.

Her plan was ruthless and while she held the guilt of killing the Admiral, she knew her mission was important. And as she came closer, she thought about her life in Lothal. How naive she was. How simple she was. Until she had a purpose.

To be someone better than she ever thought she could be.

As they entered the hundred-yard vicinity, the sailors began to notice the hull of the ship had a huge buffalo insignia on it.

'Isn't that our king's ship, captain?' the sailor came over and asked.

'No,' she lied. 'They are pirates!' she scowled and screamed. 'The pirates have taken over this ship. ATTACK! ATTACK!'

The sailors were confused, but the captain on a ship, especially the Navatakavecha's, was always right. The men would go so far as to die for their captains. And thus, the fire balls were propelled form the catapults. The enemy ship was twice in size.

She knew the fight would be useless and they would probably die.

But that was part of the plan.

Everything was in chaos.

The enemies had bigger catapults, better arrows and shields that covered their men, but Chandra didn't care about living and dying like the enemies.

She ordered her men to grab hold of the boarding planks and ordered the oarsmen to drive the ship towards the other, breaking the wood of both the hulls as they collided, making her fall on the ground, water splashing over the deck. Now there was a hole in the side of her her ship as well as her enemy's who were trying to gain control.

'BOARD IT UP!' she ordered.

And so they did, nailing the planks where holes were made. While they did so, their enemies lurched…

At their own men.

They all were part of the same gang, and yet they were fighting. Thankfully, Chandra knew that Navatakavechas were legally part of the Mahisha's group and only Mahisha and the close ones knew of this truth. To the rest of them, Navatakavechas were just a bunch of pirates.

As the attack mounted, both groups got busy. She had to run on board and before they could realise they were fighting with their comrades—she made a run for it. Sprinting across the deck, she jumped and latched onto the enemy ship as her own ship had begun to sink.

Once she was on the enemy ship, with a quick turn of her sword, she stabbed the onlookers who had come to stop her. She pierced and prodded her way through, turning back and realising her ship was keeling. Sinking. The men on it had begun to shout and cry.

And soon the people they were fighting stopped fighting and asked:

'Aren't you part of Mahisha's army?'

'We are! Who are you?'

'We are his pirates! We thought you were a ransacked ship!'

'No! We are a merchant vessel dropping important cargo for his highness.'

Oh no....

She began to run towards the lower deck, beating through the people and stabbing the ones who got in her way, as she moved to one of the cellar rooms. A man stood there, and she shoved him against the wall, punched him, and tossed him out of the round window, with all her force. She was quick as she stumbled inside the cellar and crouched there to hide in the darkness of the shadow.

She had to wait. Sweat began to gather above her eyebrows.

And she waited.

Waited...

Exhaustion seeping in.

This was very all over the place. Chaotic. Messy.

She didn't know whether she had done the right thing or not. But it was already done.

She was on the bloody ship.

She was lying down on the ground, almost asleep, before she woke up and staggered to stand up. The ship was swaying but it was on its way as she saw from the window, but when she peered out from the door she saw two soldiers who were talking:

'We have taken a quite a bit of an unnecessary hit,' one of them said.

'Well, yes we have. What was it about? I was in the kitchen while all this shit was happening.'

'Their captain basically thought this was a ship that was taken over by pirates so they were trying to save it.'

'But we didn't send any distress message.'

'Who is this captain?'

'The survivors of the ship said it was some new girl who had taken over after the Admiral died.'

'She seems fishy. Where is she?'

'We don't know. But keep an eye out. She could have died and drowned in the waters or she could be here.'

Great. So they hadn't seen her. She was quick. She went back in the corner and waited for nightfall.

The first phase of her plan was to kill the Admiral.

The second was to cause wreckage to this ship and confuse people without raising any suspicion.

The third phase was tough. Quite tough.

It was *personal.*

22

Mahisha looked at the corpse in front of him.

Trinetra was not someone he knew personally but he was *his* man and he was dead. Murdered. Stabbed multiple times. The wench was questioned but she was the one who had informed the camp by wailing and screaming. So he kept her under watch while he watched the bloody corpse. He ordered his men to take it to the border and perform the funeral rituals, while he walked outside to see Rigoli and Thamisada standing, with worried postures.

Mahisha glanced at Tabita who was with her friends in the other corner, and a lot of Panas had gathered in a circle. But now Mahisha knew it was time to get into action.

He walked to the chief and said: 'One of your people is Durga.'

'That's an accusation I wouldn't hear of, Mahisha.'

'It's *King* Mahisha,' he corrected sternly.

The chief, for a moment, stood stiffly before loosening up, 'All right. Do you want to question more than a hundred people here? Be my guest.'

'No. I want the marriage to take place in the city now.'

'What...um...but why?'

Because the city was his strength, where his army was stationed, where he could call for backup if he wanted to and he knew the secret ways and gateways of it. This was not safe. This camp. He knew of it.

'I would like to do it in the temple where I was taught to be a ruler,' Mahisha smiled placidly. Lying through his teeth.

The chief glanced worriedly at his priest and then nodded. 'Sure. Since we both have agreed to the marriage, it's best we do that, of course.'

'Great. We leave at noon.'

They had moved from the camp and towards the city. All in big huddles and groups. Mahisha was leading with Thamisada, while Tabita was sitting behind, holding him tightly. They were moving, striding slowly and he was taking turns, swivelling around in a direction that was not towards the city.

He had his reasons.

'Are you sure Mahishapur is this way?' the chief asked.

'Of course it is.'

They moved through the waters, passing through the ravines—the hooves of the horses slowly sinking into the water and splashing it. It took them time to cross. They cautiously avoided the deep foliage of the forest and exited from there, while Tabita played with the vines of the woods that were being offered. They moved out of it and were inching closer to the desert-like situation. An empty, visceral landscape of hills and sand that had no life of its own. Tabita was still clutching on to him, disregarding the fact that her father might witness their intimacy—she didn't care about it.

'I am so excited,' she whispered in Mahisha's ears.

'I am too,' he said. But he was still shaken about Trinetra.

'I'm sorry about what happened to your commander,' she said as if reading his mind.

He just stiffly nodded. He wasn't particularly happy about it either.

As they began moving, he came across a canyon with a path leading them to a camp right in the middle. A little bit of greenery dotted the place.

'What is this? Are we meeting more people?' the chief asked.

Mahisha had halted the group behind him, while he dismounted and saw that camp. It was far away and they didn't notice him now. Or maybe they had. He didn't care. He had a big army. But he definitely noticed a flag with the elephant symbol over it, a crimson flag.

It was the flag that belonged to Indra.

'It's a Deva camp,' Mahisha smiled at his new ally.

'Deva?'

'Yeah, the ones who I want you to get rid of. And this is our opportunity to defeat them. My men and Trinetra had learnt of the camp scurrying around here, in my lands, and I think it's time to fight together. In this way, we both can show our alliance to our enemies."

Rigoli glanced at the chief, who was stern and impassive in his approach. 'But we haven't even finalised the deal...'

'I think we have,' he held Tabita's hands. 'I have

agreed to marry her, and you know Mahisha's word is his promise.'

The chief was contemplating this in silence. Hundreds and hundreds of soldiers behind them. And the chief nodded. Mahisha smiled. He directed his men to move forward and they didn't even think twice. They just drove towards the horses with a frenetic energy.

Mahisha wanted the Panas to show they were also in tandem and would follow their deal through, but most of all, he wanted to see whether he could get some intelligence on Durga here.

By the time he reached in the middle of the canyon, he realised a sandstorm was incoming. The sand seeping through the crevices of the canyon didn't leave much visibility for anyone who was fighting hand-to-hand combat or archery. It was tough to figure who was who.

Mahisha knew anyone who was coming towards him was a villain. An enemy. He was in full stride, moving towards the scene with his battle axe and no armour—no shield. He didn't need anything. He was sprinting with full force when he came in front of the Deva soldier and just slammed the axe on the man's head, before the man could do anything.

Blood gushed and sprayed as the man's eyes went lifeless and he fell on the ground. Another soldier came from the back, but Mahisha kicked him hard, and the soldier flew back, crashing with a soldier who was running towards them.

Right then, two arrows pierced his back and he knelt on the ground for a moment, but he got up, pulled out the arrows, and growled like an animal. He felt like a lion being troubled by puny little hyenas.

Mahisha punched a soldier who was approaching him. Someone stabbed him in the knee from behind and he just went for a full swing of his axe and cut through the head of his enemy, flinging the head across the battlefield.

He could see sand, smell sand, and his eyes were partly closed, but he grabbed the soldier who had stabbed him, lifted him up to the sky and punched him in the larynx.

He laughed as he did it.

Mahisha picked up the axe that had fallen from his hand, and he began to move in further. On each side he could see the Panas and his men fighting the Devas. He liked how skilled these Panas were. Their skills, now at Mahisha's disposal, was worth the marriage.

A soldier came with a spear in his hand which he stabbed inside Mahisha's gut. Mahisha felt pain, but he broke the middle of the shaft of the spear with his bare hands and pulled out the leftover shaft from his stomach. With its bloody end, he stabbed the soldier repeatedly in the head, till his eyes popped out and his face was a gory mess.

Now, he saw a Deva soldier in front of him, running away at witnessing what Mahisha had just done. Mahisha casually walked behind him, with ease and control he swung his axe and brought it down against the back of the soldier, who fell on the ground. He pulled it out as the man staggered and Mahisha grabbed him by the hair, dragging him till he tugged violently on the hair pulling off the head of the soldier with a quick tug.

His eyes drew to a shadow. A shadow that was killing his men. Quick and smart with leopard-like moves. He saw the shadow move through the storm and as it came closer he found it had long hair, like a woman.

'Durga,' he gritted his teeth.

Her face was obscured by the heavy storm that was all over, but he began to move towards her.

Durga vanished instantly in the storm. He looked around, his face was pale, his fingers clasped around the axe tightly.

Thoughts began to crowd him. How did she just escape? Why did she attack him now? How did she find him?

He had found the Deva camp himself, and yet Durga had reached here.

As he was muddled in these thoughts, the figure appeared out of nowhere and struck its feet against his head, a sword in her hand. She was about to stab him when Mahisha grabbed her by the foot and tossed her inside the sandstorm. The figure, Durga, vanished yet again.

He licked his lips. She was using the environment to her advantage.

He grabbed the fallen shield and held it next to his body for any incoming attacks and...

Again out of nowhere!

Mahisha used his shield as a defence, and deflected the attack, toppling Durga to the ground.

She came on her feet, in plain sight, but there was sand and shadows and his eyes were stinging, his breathing was harsh.

The woman got up and instead of running, knelt down and instantly attacked him on the feet. He fell back and rolled over, as a dagger came close to him. He grabbed hold of the woman's weak arms and twisted it. There was a loud, familiar groan, as with his twisted dagger, he stabbed Durga in the eye. Blood sprayed over his face, as Durga moved out of the shadows and showed her face.

He knew her.

Durga must have used this opportunity to come out and kill his men since the storm would hide her face if she were careful. Otherwise, why bother showing up.

Anger began to bubble inside of him, as he grabbed the corpse of Durga and began to punch it. Again. And again. Till the skull broke off and the mouth was dislocated. It was the face of an unknown person. Someone unrecognisable by now. He was almost glad that Durga happened to turn up—she had had to, he supposed, since her Deva men were dying and she couldn't remain in hiding for long if she saw her men getting killed in the face of adversity. He was glad that his nightmare, the cause for Shukr's worry, the killer of Trinetra, was finally dead for good. He was relieved.

But then he saw the face. The stark reminder of never forgetting to truly look at faces.

After all, it belonged to the trustworthy eunuch Rigoli.

23

Seksh didn't want to see Asiloma for a while now.

And while he was straying away, he had learnt from his soldiers that someone had opened the gates of the outpost from inside so the nishadhs could come quickly and attack. Asiloma was on guard duty outside and was mainly making sure that there were no issues; no other bandit attacks on the outpost.

Seksh knew he should get out of there now. It was time. And he was considering it. Even though Mahisha would reach here first, he should leave a message to go to the capital city now, since these were unforeseen circumstances.

But why was he avoiding Asiloma as well as the prisoner Katya? He didn't know. He just knew that Katya had troubled him. It had made him worried. As a child, he would often be afraid of omens. He would be scared of the supernatural. The paranormal. And now for some reason, this Durga person was giving off these vibes. She was filling up Seksh's life with the most brutal acts of nature and he didn't know what to do about it.

And the only solace he found was in the food in front of him. Mutton was cut and served with boiled rice and curd. There was a host of other food items too and it was comforting to him. A plain wine in his goblet. And he was feasting on it, while two guards stayed inside as well as the cook.

He wanted company. He knew Asiloma could not be killed. He couldn't kill him. It was stupid. No matter how many people died. But the outpost was clearing up, his men had lessened, and the men who were supposed to come and cover up the outpost with their presence were nowhere to be seen. They had gotten delayed, and he was only expecting the worst.

As he was eating, he saw one of his guards entering, the iron boots clanging on the floor. Seksh looked up to see the guard had another mousy character with him, who was all shrivelled and drenched with rainwater.

'Who is this?' he asked.

'Messenger, general,' his guard said. 'From the platoon who were supposed to come.'

'What happened, boy?' Seksh softly asked the messenger, bracing himself.

'Bad news, general. Bad news. Our platoon was attacked horribly by the forest people.'

More Nishadhs. It was like Durga didn't want them to leave. He felt alienated. Afraid too, but the concept of fright was something he didn't want to confront.

'And you escaped in the nick of time. Heard of Durga being spoken about by the forest people?'

'Not really, general.'

Seksh nodded, shooing him off. As the man left, Seksh took a gulp of wine, letting it run down his throat. He looked up at his cook. 'The food is nice.'

'Thank you, my lord,' she bowed.

'Why are you bald, girl?'

She was immediately taken aback. 'I had a disease, my lord. Lost all my hair.'

'Ah. This world is a plague and we are the rats who bring it,' he spat on the floor. He was feeling unusually ruthless today. 'Tell me something, do you believe in ghosts?'

She shook her head. She was in long rags and loins, standing in the corner, barely visible in the darkness.

'When I was young, I used to have a ghost in my head.'

Sheksh was quiet for a while.

'Did you see it?'

'I felt it. It spoke to me one night. I was hysterical the next couple of weeks and then the shaman came and calmed me down.'

He shrugged. 'I always knew there are powers beyond our control, girl.'

'I feel so too. There's someone watching us.'

'A ghost is watching us?'

'The ones who watch us don't necessarily have to be ghosts.'

'So, you are a religious person? Gods...believe in Devas?'

'Oh no, sir. I don't believe in any man who calls himself a god. A god doesn't have to proclaim he is a god.'

It was a snide comment, but in his sluggish state, he was enjoying a conversation with someone as random as the cook. 'Karma comes for you. It always does. One way or another. The ghosts of your past, they always haunt you.' He was just muttering under his breath now.

And he looked up to see the curly haired woman. Right in front of her. She was standing. With the head of her lover in her hands and her face was covered in shadows. Blood dripped from the severed head and Seksh leaned back, pushing the chair away.

The cook and the guards came.

'You all right, general?'

'Yeah...yes...' he coughed, 'I just need to bloody sleep. Thank you.'

He was sweating. Terribly.

He was staring at the ceiling and his mind was swimming in confusion. He didn't feel good. He had gone to the latrine and retched multiple times. He was cold. Terribly cold but hot on the forehead. Feverish. He was just...

Ghost.

He was thinking about the ghost in his room. He looked at the apparition in the corner of his room that was staring back at him.

Was it the curly haired woman with a severed head in her palms? Was it someone else?

He couldn't see. It was all shadows.

'Tainted one, you are the curse which will be the downfall of your ruler's army,' the whisper came.

And it was similar to the ghost he had heard. He sat back down on the bed, shutting his eyes, as if doing so would help. The ghost would go away and everything would be fine.

He could feel it. The hands...they were touching him. Lingering traces felt next to him. It was icy cold.

'I am not afraid of you,' he said.

'But you should be,' the whisper came.

'No I am not. No, I am bloody not,' he was clutching on to the sword next to him. Really hard, as if he would break it. 'Leave me alone.'

'No, I won't. You'll be fine, darling. You'll be fine,' the whisper said. 'See my face. See my beautiful face and know what you fear the most.'

'I don't fear anything. Mahisha protects me.'

'He doesn't care. If he knows about you, he will kill you the moment he sees you.'

'No...*NO!*' he shrieked.

And he opened his eyes to see the apparition opening the door and leaving through it.

'I will kill you,' sweat beads were falling from his face as he began to follow the apparition.

He began to trudge in the empty corridors, he realised the corridors were moving. They had mouths and faces of strange men, laughing at him.

'You like men. What a tainted soul you are!'

'Mahisha will kill you if he knows your secret.'

'KILL ASILOMA BEFORE MAHISHA KILLS HIM. THE BLOODSHED AT THE HANDS OF THE LOVER IS NOT MURDER!'

All these voices. He fell down. He heard a sound from the corridors. Echoes. And then something rolled down.

It was the same severed head of the man he had killed. A boy's, in fact.

'Get away!' he screamed, pushing himself back.

And as he turned...

The lady in white was standing. Blood dripping from her too. Her eyes white as the moon, just watching him. 'Kill Asiloma.'

'No, no, I won't.'

'Then kill your fears.'

'Where...how...'

She pointed to the door. Next to the corridor. He began to scurry forward. Kicked it open. Sweat came out of his pores as he saw the apparition lying on the bed. As if he was sleeping. But it was right there. The ghost who had been haunting him ever since his childhood.

It was right there on the bed. He brought the sword next to the apparition.

'Whoever you are, I shall kill you, you filthy...'

And the face turned. Sheksh saw what he feared the most.

Himself.

It was his face and for a moment, Seksh was confused.

'No...but...'

'You were always afraid of yourself. You always thought you were a killing machine. You always thought you were just a crazy nutjob. That's your fear. To be the worst version of yourself,' his apparition replied.

'But am I not a good man?'

'Perhaps in your nightmares.' And the apparition chuckled.

Seksh, in absolute fury, brought down the blade and stabbed the apparition. Multiple times. Again. Again. Till there was nothing left and Seksh felt relief.

I have killed it. I have done it. Yes. Finally.

He went to the window in the room. Trying to shake

things off. Trying to feel a certain sort of pleasure in knowing he had finally won. He could feel the air and the wind gratifying him, making him think clearly, and the blurry vision went away after a while. He retched once more, before he turned to see the apparition who he had killed.

But instead, it was all blood. So much of it. Everywhere.

He walked to it. Staggering. And he saw the apparition.

It was lying on the bed. Sprawled.

It didn't have his face anymore.

In fact…

Seksh cried loudly. *NO.*

It was the one face he desperately didn't want to see there.

Asiloma.

24

Gauri was tied up in the prison, with one small window that overlooked the city. The window was small, but without grills, gratefully.

Her hands and legs were bound with a tight rope. From the shadows of the corner of her cell, she sensed someone entering. Shukr. He was looking defeated and disappointed, surprisingly.

'You always astound me,' he said slowly.

He had guards behind him.

Gauri was surprised she still hadn't been executed. But perhaps, her luck was now running out as behind the disappointed gaze of her master, was barely contained fury.

'You shouldn't have taken the child,' he said. 'He was ours.'

Gauri remained quiet.

'Why are you doing this?'

She didn't respond.

'Are you troubled by how we function? I thought you were such a talented person when I first got you on board and now look at you. A complete rebel.'

Silence.

'Fine,' he sighed, coming close to the grills. 'I will not bear any of this, any longer. You stay here as long as you get so frustrated that you cry to return to your normal life. But if you mess up after this, that'll be the end of the rope. I will not forgive you any longer.'

And with that he began to leave when Gauri cleared up her throat and asked: 'Why are you not killing me?'

He didn't turn back, but said: 'There are things beyond your understanding, girl.'

And after saying that, he left.

The moment he did, the guards left as well. She counted how many rotations the prison guard did and when the count was done...

She came into action.

She tried to bring her knotted arms underneath her legs and with a quick shove, broke the bounds. Then she untied her legs. When she was done, she began to move quickly for the window.

She realised she was in the tall tower, adjacent to the palace and it was tough for her to escape by just jumping—she could fall to death.

But she did have a plan.

The guard would be coming any second.

With a quick shove of her body, she lurched out of the window and grabbed the ledge as tight as possible. She waited for the guard to come.

As expected, the guard noticed the bounds were broken. Shocked, he entered the prison by unlocking it.

He went to check the window, and when Gauri saw him, she grabbed him by the collar, pulling him down and throwing him off the window.

She climbed back up and dusted off her clothes before she made her way to her companions.

Gauri had knocked on all the doors. She had made sure that everyone knew she had escaped and they had all gathered—twenty or so female slaves in the common hall of their corridor. She had managed the guards along the way. Many women hadn't wanted to accompany her for she was known as a a troublemaker, but she convinced them. One last opportunity to talk to them and then she would leave.

As they waited in the corridor, Gauri squared onto them. She saw the innocent face of Airavati as well as the brutish face of Mata and the other girls.

'I apologise for my behaviour which has brought all of you under scrutiny these last couple of days but I really want to talk about something,' she began. 'And this is the last time. I won't speak after this or trouble you. We have lived under the boot of our oppressors for the longest time and today I want your support. I have been with you all since the beginning and I feel we are the ones who can go out there and fight.'

'But how?' Airavati asked. 'We have no weapons.'

'We don't need weapons. We just need to do one thing to shape the public's opnion.'

'And why should we do it?' Mata asked. 'Frankly, we are enjoying our lives.'

'Really? We are servants. We can't have an independent life. We do what others tell us to do. But the most important thing is, we can't do what we want to do—we can't have a family, we can't fall in love or have children. We do what they tell us to do. All the time.'

They all had begun to nod and agree, while some remained static.

'Why choose us?' another girl asked. 'Why not anyone else?'

'Because as a family, I only have you. No matter how much you hate me, I belong with you all,' she paused, feeling emotional. 'I've done a few things in the past out of insubordination because I wanted to show you that it can be done. That small actions can lead to big effects,' she paused. 'Sheena...' she asked one girl in the corner, 'do you remember how you were forced by Mahisha to actually cook the entire day a perfect meal just because he didn't like what you made first? Veena...' she turned to the other one, 'remember how you were thrown down the stairs when they learnt you had an affair with a mopper? They made sure you couldn't have a child. For no good reason. Remember Airavati, how you are always made a table, because well...they just can. And Mata...remember how you are called in front of the ministers just so you could make them laugh and light up their day? You aren't a jester. We are treated like objects. Always. That's the saddest part.'

'And what is your plan?' Mata stepped up. 'To basically dismantle a regime that has been here since the last two decades? How do you plan to do it? It's practically impossible!'

'We need the public on our side,' Gauri said. 'We need them to believe in what is right. And how, you ask? By doing what the rules tell us not to do. We should go inside the temple where women aren't allowed in and we should break down the statue of Mahishasura.'

For a moment, they all went silent, for they couldn't believe that she had just said that.

'This action of ours,' Gauri added, 'would make the people believe that they aren't worshipping a god, they are worshipping a man, a stone structure.'

'And if we get caught? We can die!' cried Mata.

'And what are we doing here, frankly speaking? We are already dead, moved by force and nothing else. You know, this...this bullying towards us has become so normal that we rationalise it and feel lucky that we are here. But it's not true. We deserve better,' Gauri sighed. 'It's your choice, after all. Do you want to do it or not?'

None of them looked certain for some reason. They all had faced some sort of problem under this system for sure. But there was a glimmer of hope. And each one of them began to nod. Finally, Mata said: 'Fine. Let's do the deed, let's make people believe in themselves more than the king. I hope we don't die, Gauri.'

'I have everything in control. I'll figure out a way to make sure we don't die,' Gauri smiled, as all the women came together and hugged each other.

Gauri smiled at Airavati, who embraced her separately.

'So what now?' Mata asked.

Gauri knew the ins and outs of the palace. They had to take down the statue in the early morning. Tomorrow would be the seventh day and it would be perfect. She also knew she needed weapons. She had to plan out a way for more than twenty women to escape. The tunnel was there, and it was perfect.

'Mata, you go for the underground cellar and get rid of the guards there. Your weapons could be anything ranging from a pair of...'

'You don't have to tell me about weapons, girl,' she grinned as she slapped her muscles. 'I can knock them out the way I want to.'

'Great. Clear the underground tunnel and since there are so many of you, you can take on the sewer guards easily. We can escape through the sewers. But the temple we are trying to attack does have a certain number of guards.'

'Almost twenty,' Airavati added, 'which means we need proper weapons.'

'How many people know how to use a weapon here?' Gauri asked.

None of them raised their hands except for Mata.

'Great,' Gauri sighed. 'Let us get the weapons,' she signalled to Airavati and herself, 'and then I have a plan to distract the guards there. Our agenda is not to kill those guards, but to incapacitate the statue. That's our first priority.'

All the girls nodded.

Gauri smiled. Her mission was finally coming to fruition.

'Let's do it, everyone.'

25

Tamar was in the room sitting next to Sulochna, holding her hand and kissing her on the forehead. He was worried for her. Sure. And he was hugging her. She was still distraught. The day had passed by and he hadn't talked to her much after that. He wanted to give her space before she could reveal more about the confession she had made. He couldn't believe it was Shukr, but then one didn't know anything.

Bashkala was found dead. With two guards. No reason. It was on the outskirts of the city. An investigation was already on, since the deaths left no trace of another person there. And why would anyone want to kill Tamar's personal captain? It didn't make sense.

His life was falling apart, but his eyes were glued to his wife.

'Do you want something to eat? Shall I bring you dinner?'

'He said he did it because I was a liability in your life,' Sulochna said, sighing. 'I don't know why he thought that,' she was trying to push out words, weeping throughout. 'Do you think I am?'

'Of course not, dear,' he paused. 'So he kidnapped you? Then why the ransom and that trial?'

'He wanted people to turn against you. So your

influence wanes off. He can't just kick you out. You are Mahisha's close friend.'

'And he's my guru, but...' he was confused.

'I don't think he cares. He's a strategist, as you have always told me. He must have something up his sleeve. Perhaps wants to be the Prime Minister himself, I don't know.'

Tamar was so confused. It didn't sound like Shukr at all. But then he did remember that Shukr was after the position of the minister before Mahisha gave it to him. What happened was, Mahisha had gotten so powerful once he became the ruler that he decided to stop caring what Shukr had taught him and did what he had to do. Of course, experience had made him tougher and stronger than usual. Perhaps that's why he wanted to keep Shukr as just a reminder of the past, a respect for his teacher, that was it.

'Okay, it's fine. I should talk to him.'

'Don't,' she rasped. 'It'll only make things worse. You must do something, take revenge, I don't know...' she was being hysterical and he hugged her tightly.

They remained quiet for the longest time and perhaps hours had gone by when he heard something. And quick as a flash, a ball of fire just broke into his house.

For a moment, they were stunned, and Tamar left the wide-eyed Sulochna to see the ball was a rock wrapped with animal fat that was put on fire.

Who threw it, though?

People were yelling outside. For long. Tamar came out of his palace to find more than a hundred men had gathered and they were throwing rocks and all kinds of other stuff. It was all over the damn place, as balls of fire were breaking through the windows and hitting his men...

One came straight towards him, hitting his head and breaking the headpiece he was wearing.

Tamar fell, and Sulochna rushed to help him.

'This is not going well. I'll order for more security tomorrow,' he said.

Sulochna added: 'Why can't you just...'

'Kill them? It'll be a massacre.' He shook his head.

The next day as he was writing for sanctions and allowances for more security in his common hall—special security to be given to get rid of the rioters who were on the streets making noise—he found a familiar figure stepped in and shut the ornate, golden door close behind.

Tamar looked up to find the blotchy, ragged-haired man with loose skin and saggy eyes. He was in his grey robe today and he was looking awfully dull and exhausted.

'Guruji,' he said and even though he didn't want to, contempt had begun to seep through his mouth through his tone.

'I heard what's happening with you,' Shukr said. 'In what mind did you think of...well, killing those men?'

You made me do it, Tamar wanted to say but he was quiet. He was a genuinely patient man, but his patience was waning thin. 'I had my reasons.'

'And those were?'

'They were wrong.'

'Do you know every street is filled with those rioters? What do you plan to do about them?'

'I am creating task forces that'll imprison them.'

'You can't possibly try to imprison all the men of the city.'

I can give it a try.

'That's the only way. In fact...' he signed the scroll with his quill and ordered the man from outside to come inside and take it so it could be enforced. 'For a while at least.'

Shukr couldn't believe it for a moment. He stood there as the order of imprisoning the rioters—which would be half the men of the city to be put behind bars—was frankly stupid. But it was the only way to condemn the violence that was haunting the streets and threatening the Prime Minister.

'There's another way,' Shukr said.

'What?'

'I know you won't like it.'

'Humour me,' Tamar said. He knew what was coming.

'You can step down from the position of the Prime Minister.'

There it was. His wife was right. 'Why?'

'Everyone hates you right now. It's best this position to be left vacant till Mahisha comes and—'

Tamar didn't hear further. He went to the door and said, 'Thanks for offering the suggestion but I believe I won't step down.'

Shukr sighed. He staggered out of the door and gave one look of fury before moving out.

Tamar had a hard time believing his wife for he trusted his guru but when he said it....it was all clear. He was the one who kidnapped her. He wanted him to get displaced as the Prime Minister.

Grunting under his breath, he knew Mahisha was on his way to the city. And hopefully things would get better then.

Sulochna was wiping her kohl, which was smeared all over her cheeks. She wiped her face and then freshened herself up when she heard the voice:

'You are quite an actress.'

Sulochna, for a moment, was dumbfounded that the person had come into her private chambers, but then she played it cool. 'I always had the knack for theatrics.'

'Good. I'm glad you went with the plan and did what was necessary.'

'I hope you know what you are doing,' Sulochna said. 'Because yesterday a rock fell inside and Tamar was inside. I don't want both of us dead. I only did it because it was the right thing to do and Tamar is a good man.'

'He has to show that he's open to changes,' the voice said. 'When the time comes.'

Sulochna didn't know how her husband would react and whether he would change or not. But she turned to see the person.

And saw the one who orchestrated everything, the one who had convinced Sulochna to get herself kidnapped, to hide in a particular place for a while and then blame all of it on Shukr—

It was Charini.

26

Chandra was waiting inside a cellar for an entire day and by the following day's nightfall, she was starving. The soldiers had come in the cellar, but in low numbers and she was hidden in the corner like a mouse. She would have the tidbits of cheese, that she had managed to carry in her pouch, to keep her stomach a tad bit full.

And once she saw the half moon through the tiny window, she made a move outside of the cellar, realising someone was right there sleeping at night. She brought a dagger close to his throat and slit it, and without him even screaming, the blood poured out and the man died.

She began to move further, tiptoeing towards the captain's cabin, hoping to meet him.

She knew she had to. As she manoeuvered the darkness, she saw a guard whistling in the corridor. She was standing right on the ledge, waiting for him to make a turn and when he was just about to...

He stopped. Picking his teeth.

With a clenched jaw, Chandra waited, exasperated. Her breathing was strong. And when the man didn't make the turn but moved towards where he was coming from—Chandra moved to his back and plunged the dagger into his spine bringing her free hand over his mouth. There was a short scream which was lost in the darkness. The man fell on the ground, dying.

Chandra, crouching, moved forward, passing the

kitchen which she saw was empty for now. Most sailors were sleeping and others would have been on the deck, keeping an eye for an enemy ship. But Chandra was inside, as they would have never anticipated.

She came towards the captain's lodge and realised—this was it. This was the moment she was waiting for.

She remembered how she never wanted to come be a part of this revolution for something she was emotional about. But she remembered one thing that starkly changed her perception and made her be part of this mission.

It was five years ago. Before she had met the Deva Varuna.

She had returned to Lothal port after running from it and while she was hoping everything would have been fine there—it wasn't. The beautiful landscape was broken into pieces. Fire was raging and civilians were killed. They didn't just murder the ones who were under the gramani, they murdered everyone who was in their way, while others had been made prisoners.

She sneaked inside the city, missing the vision of the soldiers who were doing the rounds and she saw the wharf where her shack used to be. And she began to wander, for reasons she herself was unsure about. Perhaps she was hoping to find some sort of reasoning that this mayhem and chaos happened for the right reasons, but so much of bloodshed was not necessary.

Her eyes fell over a corpse she knew very well and as she came closer, she saw who it was.

Bikram. The young porter who she treated like her young brother. He was beaten mercilessly, and he lay amidst the rest of the porter friends of his. She knelt down, weeping, and hoping none of the guards would see her.

She touched his hair, when she saw there was something in his hands. She opened his palm to see a bitten apple.

He had finally bought and eaten his food from the money Chandra had given him. A smile, so tragic, swept over her face.

'My men were sure they saw someone enter. A shadow perhaps, but didn't know it was a little girl,' a voice came. Smooth. Soft. Charming.

She turned to see the same boy she had seen at the port. Tall. Handsome. With the sharp definite face and shoulder length hair that would rival the gods of Greek sailors.

Durmukha, as Bikram had called him.

'What are you doing here, girl?' he asked.

She didn't say anything. She just looked at him. With a careful gaze. And he looked back at her. He was with his guards, behind, ready to catch her if she tried to escape.

'I have come to take my brother,' she said.

Durmukha nodded. 'Do you plan to tell anyone about this little work of art of ours?'

She shook her head vigorously.

'Good. Good. But alas, I can't take you on your word. So...' he snapped his fingers.

She screamed and began to scamper as quickly as

she could, moving for the wharf, holding the boy in her hand. It was only making her lag behind, and she kept running. As far as possible. The men following her. Everything had begun to feel dazed.

And she had fallen in the water, as arrows came slithering in the ocean but not hitting her. But the deep fall led her to loosen her grip on Bikram's corpse and he was gone deep into the waters. She tried to get it, but she had a hard time swimming so deep and thus she floated away from the wharf.

And away from everything.

Chandra opened the captain's lodges and in front of her, she saw what she was expecting to see. What it was all about. All the mission practices she did. She lied to herself when she said it wasn't about anything personal. It was about something more. It was about showing her enemies that bitterness and the hatred always returned in bountiful.

And she saw Durmukha sitting on his table, in front of her, unaware a girl had just entered. He still had that charming face, the one she had seen five years back and five years had been kind on him. He looked youthful.

He looked up.

'Yes? Did I call for you?' he asked. He was scribbling something on the parchments. 'Do I know you?'

She just stood there for a moment.

'Are you from the kitchen? What happened? Rats?' He stood up, frustrated. 'It's always the bloody rats.'

He stood. And she stood in silence.

And then he looked at her. Her eyes. He felt it had a deep resonance.

'Do you remember Lothal?' she asked.

He was frozen. 'No.'

'Do you remember me?' she pulled out her dagger. And he realised he was at a disadvantage. His sword was on the side of the table, but she came close and she had already thrown the sword on the floor.

'The girl from Lothal.'

'Frankly, lass, I don't remember that day. I was...I was filled with adrenaline and I am sorry if I-I-I hurt you,' he was whimpering, getting cornered. 'I hadn't meant to do whatever I did.'

She shoved him in the back and brought the knife, stabbing him on the shoulder and closing his mouth, so his scream was short and low. For a moment, he was shocked by what she had just done and then she said: 'That's for not even bothering to remember me. I want something from you.'

'What? Is it the gold I'm carrying? You can take it.'

'Oh no. That's just the tip of the iceberg. I want the entire mountain,' she grinned. 'If you value your life.'

'What is it?'

'Mahisha's treasury, unlike other empires', is scattered across Southern Jambudvipa. In caves, guarded, or in small forts. They are in the unlikeliest of places and that's smart because the enemies would always attack the capital hoping the treasury to be there, but it isn't, and they are on a fool's errand. That's it, wasn't it?'

He was nodding frantically.

'Good. So you tell me about those places and I'll let you live.'

'For Mahisha to kill me. Oh no, thank you very much. Might as well die by your hands.'

She cut a vein on his neck which began to bleed and he held it by his hands growing pale, and said: 'I have cut your carotid artery. You have about two minutes to tell me, before I tell you how to stop yourself from getting killed.'

'Please...please...'

'You can either die today or you can hide from Mahisha. He's going down, so you don't have to worry.'

'Who are you?'

She didn't say anything. She brought him a parchment and a quill, made him write the names of the places where the treasury was divided. He did it slowly, as much as he could, with blood from his neck spraying a bit on the parchment. And finally, when he was done with it, she snatched it from his palms.

'How can I stop the bleeding? Tell me.'

'I don't even know what artery I have cut. You aren't dying,' she chuckled, as his eyes grew wide with fury.

'This was your plan, eh? Just to ask me this. How did you come on this ship? Ah, I know. The attack by the Navatakavechas. But why do it on the ship? I'm mostly on land. You could have apprehended me there. I'm just...I'm just curious.'

She thought about it. The Devas had told her to plan according to what seemed best. They just trained her and guided her.

'Because when your treasuries would be getting

looted, you wouldn't have the time to inform Mahisha when you are on the ship. Now it will take you a whole lot of time. And that is what I needed. Time.'

She had become a part of the Navatakavechas because it was easier to get on that with no past than to get on a vessel of Durmukha's or any of the other legal ships since each sailor's background was listed in detail, and she didn't have a background in sailing. But she knew that Durmukha did a lot of off sea travelling to discuss foreign relations for his empire, get money, send money. Meet people on behalf of Mahisha. She knew she had to get on the ship while it was on water as the treasuries would have to be hit in time before Mahisha or anyone close to him was informed about it. Once the treasuries were looted, Mahisha would get to know, but it would be too late by then.

'I'll send the fastest bloody messenger and a horse when I land on the shores, you fucking bitch,' he yelled at Chandra. 'Mahisha will know before you attack these places and you won't be able to do anything.'

'Of course. But that is *if* you land,' she smiled, and then she stabbed him straight in the head, so he couldn't notify the others. He bled profusely. His body was then pushed under the table, so the guards wouldn't notice him.

And then she began to move for the final phase of her plan.

While she was indeed in the cellar, she wasn't there just to find refuge. For the day and a half that she was in, she had been trying to find the barrels which contained poison for the arrows and she had a rope made of animal fat that she tied to the barrels. It was quite long. She ignited the rope with the fire torches that hung in the corridors.

She found a spare boat, that she sat down in and began to pulley herself down to the waters. It was close to the main deck, and a guard came to her, asking: 'What are you doing?'

She confidently said, 'Catching fish. I'm the cook.'

The guard was confused. 'You can't just do that here. You need permission to use the boat so we can halt the ship.'

'You can talk to the captain for that. I don't care. I am just doing what I've been told.'

The guard was suspicious and he ordered her to stay while he confirmed with the captain. While she sat there, she saw the other guards looking at her. All of them.

Chandra smiled and then left the pulley. The boat strung down as fast as it could, the pulley breaking and the boat splashed against the water.

'It's almost...'

And there was an explosion. A huge explosion at the rear end of the ship. It wouldn't break the ship completely but would slow them down while they sent a distress signal.

She began to oar herself out of the damage, as she saw the destination. Few miles ahead there was a coast.

And then she would be off to the rendezvous point.

27

Close to the outskirts of Mahishapur, they had set up camp to rest. The horses were drawn and tired, so were the people. It was a short journey, but there were quite a few detours along the way. One being fighting with the Devas and winning over them, the other being going to the outpost where Seksh was. Mahisha wanted to meet his friend and know exactly which Durga he had caught, since the Durga that he had killed, was someone else.

And it was confusing. Definitely.

Mahisha was in his tent, drinking his wine, and Tabita was massaging his shoulders, trying to make him forget the worries of his life.

'I really didn't know Rigoli would turn out to be Durga.'

But was he really? Mahisha just didn't know. Seksh said something else.

'But did your father know?' he asked.

'No, of course not, dear.'

Mahisha flared his nostrils. He came on his feet, shoving her hand away from his shoulder and squaring up to her. His eyes met hers.

'Tell me the truth.'

'I-I...' her innocent eyes blinked.

'Women tend to lie through their teeth,' he growled as he grabbed Tabita by the throat and lifted her up.

She was choking. Going red.

'Tell me the truth, girl.'

Tabita couldn't even speak but she was still shaking her head. Denying.

Mahisha looked at her weasel face and then tossed her in the corner, out of anger. He was frustrated. He didn't know what to feel.

'I have nothing to do with this, your highness,' she said, almost weeping now.

But the distant liking he had for her had vanished. Mahisha was angry. Furious. And then his eyes sharply drew to the person who entered his tent. It was none other than Thamisada. He glanced at his daughter and then back at Mahisha.

'Is everything okay Tabita?' he asked.

She nodded. Coughing. 'Of course, was feeling unwell.'

Thamisada nodded and turned to Mahisha. 'Shall we move?'

'How did you not know about Rigoli?' Mahisha snapped.

'He was a trusted man, as far as I know. I never saw him correspond with the Devas.'

'And yet he did,' Mahisha growled. 'And he made up that stupid prophecy that Durga is here to scare me off. Perhaps he didn't want the deal between us to happen.'

Thamisada nodded. 'That could be it.'

And he thought Mahisha would run away after hearing the prophecy, but instead he was okay with it. He wasn't scared. But knowing what he knew about

Durga—it meant, he was a spy in Thamisada's army. For sure. Otherwise, how would he have known about Durga?

Nine days. He remembered what Shukr had told him. By calculations, today was the eighth day. Tomorrow he was supposed to die and yet he was around all his army and no one could touch him.

His guard interrupted their conversation and said: 'He's speaking, my lord.'

Thamisada was confused. Mahisha grinned.

'Let's see what he has to say.'

In the battle with the Devas, Mahisha had rounded up their soldiers who were then tortured to reveal the truth about Durga. About anything related to an attack on him, since he realised that she was playing smart with him. The interrogation had lasted a day and most of them died, except for one who was now shrivelling like a leaf in chilly winter in front of Mahisha. He was stabbed, cut, and wounded so he would reveal all the details that were important.

The torturer, Mahisha, and Thamisada were here in the empty tent.

'Tell me. What do you know?'

'It's almost a decade long program,' the man said, crying. 'About killing you.'

'In nine days, yes?'

'Yes, but it's more than that.'

'What do you mean?'

The solider looked up; his face creased with blood. 'It's about taking down your empire.'

Mahisha chuckled. 'But it was about assassinating me. We got a letter...'

'That was part of the plan,' he said. 'You were supposed to get a letter that would alarm you but the Devas knew you wouldn't take it seriously.'

'Why?'

'To plant an idea that you would be assassinated when in fact, it was not the case. Your assassination is the last priority. First is to destabilise your power and control.'

Mahisha grabbed the soldier's head as he was beginning to pass out. 'What else, man?'

'It's...it's...'

'Who is Durga?'

He shook his head. 'No one knows. But what we do know is that there are four women working in your system. They are operating under Durga. They work for Durga. These four women were under different names, guises and identities working their way up the social system of your empire, so they could crumple it from inside when the Nine Nights would begin.'

'That's the operation's name?'

He nodded.

'Do you know about the Scythian Rigoli who was part of it? A eunuch?'

'He could be working under Durga, but he's not Durga. He could also be a paid assassin by the Devas to make you think that it's Durga, so you feel secured that you know who Durga is.'

But the Devas didn't anticipate Seksh sending him a letter which said he had caught Durga. This would make their plan null and void. Mahisha grinned. Unknowingly, his friend had just made him feel secure.

'Any idea who Durga is? Think hard.'

'No.' The soldier swallowed bile. 'I just know one last thing. You should leave for your capital as soon as possible if you want to save it.'

Mahisha nodded. And realising he had nothing more to offer, with quick force, he pulled out the man's head from his body by just his brute strength. The headless body collapsed while the severed head stared back at him lifelessly. 'You are the first Deva soldier who I actually ended up liking.'

He smiled and turned to Thamisada. 'Let's meet this next Durga, I suppose.'

28

Seksh had done the antyeshi for his lover and he cried the entire time. He couldn't believe he had killed his own lover because of some hallucinations. But how was he getting them? He had no idea. He was angry about it. He had no clue what was going on. His mind was just on a trip. Omens surrounded him and they were glaring at him to now kill himself. He wanted to kill himself, but he knew Mahisha would be on his way.

Was it Katya's strange powers that made him hallucinate and think he was killing a ghost of his past rather than his lover who was sleeping in the other room?

Seksh was confused. And his only solace was the food that was given to him. The cook was yet again standing there but he had no guards anymore. She was serving him, while he was feasting, hoping it would make him forget what he had done to Asiloma. He was crying in bouts when he said what he was thinking loudly:

'I'm going to kill her today,' he drank his wine. 'I'll kill Katya or Durga or whoever she is. I don't care if Mahisha shows up and he's not able to interrogate her. I don't care. It's because of her. All because of her.'

'Whatever you wish, my lord,' she said.

Seksh looked up at the cook, and he grabbed her hands. 'Your hands are the only thing that makes me feel like it's worth living. I have begun to crave your food more and more and it's what comforts me.'

'Thank you for your kind words, my lord.'

He looked at her hands. Continued to do so. They were a bit burnt, he realised. And had a patch on it. 'How did you burn yourself? When was this?'

She pulled them away from him as she thoughtfully said, 'Probably during the time you had burnt my hut.'

'What?'

Seksh looked up. Confused.

The cook sighed. 'You had lit up our hut with fire. Me and my friend, we tried to escape. You entered. You killed him. And I was able to run away from you.'

'No...no...' he shook his head, 'are you...how do you know about my dreams?'

'It's not your dreams. You have done it a long time back,' she smiled placidly. She looked weak. 'It's me. Khushi, the potter who Mahisha, your king, wanted to woo.'

'No...no...'

'Yes.'

He tried to grab her, but she stepped further away and Seksh fell on the ground, coughing loudly and feeling his stomach had some worms inside. 'What...I'm so confused. You had curly hair?'

'I went bald so you wouldn't recognise me.'

'But...' he was weeping now. 'Why do I feel strange? Did you...'

'Yes, I poisoned you. Just like how I slipped Soma inside your drink yesterday and dressed up as a ghost to aggravate your hallucinations, guiding you to kill Asiloma. Katya and I thought you would have listened to us by just the omens, but you still held your ground.

You didn't want to kill him, so we resorted to more trickery.'

'Why?' he coughed.

'Because you killed my lover. And because you are the general. You cut the head off the army and the army has no idea who they should follow.'

'Mahisha will...'

She smiled, kneeling down. 'You should worry about yourself now. When Mahisha comes, he will see a picture that we want him to see: A deranged general who murdered his lieutenant and then killed himself. It'll be a nice picture, won't it?'

That is why.

It was to leave no trace.

'No, don't...I beg of you...'

'I do have the antidote, if you want,' she showed him the vial. 'Do you want to drink it and survive?'

He looked at it. It was barter. 'What do you want in return?'

'Blueprints of the capital. Tell me where all the gates are.'

'So you can tell the Devas from where to enter?'

'They already have an idea about the gates, but it would be better if you told me, it would mean less hassle.'

He sighed.

'You are a good man, Seksh. You did what you were told to do,' Khushi said. 'Don't let your last breaths be wasted on Mahisha, who has committed such horrible crimes that we had to come and do this. Asiloma would have survived if Mahisha wouldn't have told you to kill my friend in that hut that day. Think about it. It's a domino effect.'

Seksh looked up and he could see his life ebbing away. He could see how he was taught to follow Mahihsa; the ruthless leader. He could see how he defied Mahisha one time by falling in love with Asiloma. And he could see...his past life coming back to him. Ghosts. His ghost was he himself. Even though it was orchestrated by Khushi, it was him.

Realising he had to redeem himself from the most glorious and the most horrible crimes that he had committed on behalf of Mahisha, he told her about the gates and she listened. He told her how many outposts there were and she listened, and by the end of it, she gave him the vial.

'If you promise me to not follow us.'

He nodded. And he took the wine. She left the room and he knew that Khushi would go to Katya and rescue her from the prison and they would leave before Mahisha came. He knew all of that.

But he smiled, as he looked at the antidote.

And he broke it into pieces.

The antidote seeping into the ground.

Seksh knew that he had lived his life. Enough. It was not worth living anymore.

29

Gauri and Airavati were casually walking to the armoury, with Gauri covering her face a bit with a shawl. Airavati walked up to the guard, who was in front of the palace armoury and said:

'There's been a bit of a mishap. Guru Shukr is looking for you on the top floor.'

'Guruji? But me? Why?'

'He wants more guards at his disposal. Something has come up,' she said.

The guard looked at them suspiciously and then was about to say something when Gauri used her elbows to smack him in the nose, making him unconscious.

'I really don't have time for this guy. They have already left for the sewers. So we should run too,' Gauri said, referring to her band of rioters.

They entered the armoury and it was obviously small since it wasn't the national armoury where the weapons were welded and created. This was used during emergencies and they went with a sack and tried to get as many small weapons for themselves as they could. When they were full, Airavati asked:

'How would we kill the guards? We have no combat training.'

Gauri clenched her jaw. She was hoping that Charini, her ally, would have caused the controversial hearing to happen, leading to men rioting and creating chaos in the streets. This would give the city guards something else to worry about rather than staying in huge numbers at the temple. But she could only hope. 'Let's see what we can do. I'm sure I'll figure out a way to—'

'Be clever again?' a voice came.

Both girls turned to face Shukr who was standing there. But with two guards behind him, aiming their arrows at her and Airavati.

'And you thought I would let you escape so easily, since it was clear that you had escaped the prison and my men were following around the likes of you, and they caught a sight of you in this corridor,' Shukr said. 'Why do you do this, Gauri? I'm just dumbfounded. And now since, you have left me with no choice...kill the other one and leave Gauri to me,' he ordered.

'Why don't you ever kill me?' Gauri asked, through clenched teeth. 'What is it that stops you? This is the third time I have made a mistake and by now I should have been stabbed thrice. So, what is it?'

Shukr stood there for a moment. He didn't order the guards with the snap of his fingers. 'Because I have a feeling...' he said with a pause, 'that you are my granddaughter and you were taken away by the Devas.'

Gauri stood there in silence. The sack she was holding on to slipped from her hands. She didn't know what to feel.

She was frozen and she could see he was feeling triumphant. He felt he had gained control over her again. Mentally. Emotionally. Even though it was supposed to be an emotional reunion, there was something strange and sinister behind why this information was conveyed to her.

'Ah, I know,' he smiled, 'You are my blood and you are meant to be my successor. You are just misguided. You didn't know it was me and now when you do, I know you will come around.'

'What makes you think I didn't know?' Gauri said.

That made him pause. Shukr arched his brows.

'I ran away from you because I wanted to. I joined the Devas because I wanted to. I was tired of living with you. You were crazy. You were controlling. And when I learnt I could be working under you, I was happy. I knew what you had done to the empire, to the people, the crimes you had committed, and I was horribly shocked and ashamed. And I knew I wanted to do the right thing. To be here, under you, was a choice, not chance.'

Shukr was taken aback.

'But I am just glad,' she added, 'that you have known about me,' she saw shadows coming behind the guards and knocking them out. It was Mata and one more slave. They must have come here since Gauri and Airavati hadn't returned to the sewers till now.

Shukr was helpless. He knelt down. Begging with clasped hands. Gauri brought out the axe from the sack and held it up.

'You know now,' she said, as she severed the guru's head, his blood spraying on her face, 'that you have been killed by your blood.'

By the time they had reached the temple, after escaping from the sewers, Gauri realised that many of the men had been put behind bars and women were walking on the streets without fear. It was a fresh change, to see things like this. And around the temple, of course, the women walked, but they weren't entering.

Gauri and her entire band of emancipated women had weapons, each carrying them on themselves, and she saw that thankfully the guards were less in number. Probably five. Two outside the gate, and three inside. And they were twenty women. The reinforcements would come, if someone announced it.

'What's the plan?' Mata asked, as they walked towards the gates.

Gauri was thinking how to distract them, but she was done playing in the shadows. She wanted to go all out and upfront about it. 'We fight.'

'But we don't know how to.'

'Channel the anger in you and swish your swords and daggers. It's not that tough,' Gauri said. It was almost a bit funny what she said, since there was definitely a method to fighting, but she knew she would take care of the five herself.

She began to run towards the guards, who noticed the band of women in white clothes rushing towards them. They were confused for a moment...

But not for long. Gauri instantly slammed her axe across the guard's face, slashing his cheeks and nose, while kicking the other one to the ground. The women entered behind her, and they all began to attack.

The women on the streets began to come together

to see what was happening. The riots had begun again. A different one this time.

The guards were astounded but Mata fuelled her hatred through her actions towards these guards as she used her sword to stab and impale them. Airavati was herself afraid though, and she didn't know what to do with her dagger but was imitating Mata. A guard lurched at her, as she fell on the ground. She tried to get rid of him, but he was going to stab her when Mata kicked him and helped her get up. They both grinned at each other.

Gauri ran towards the statue and began to cut through it with her axe. With each cut she made, she looked at her band of women who had taken down the guards now. She had cut the feet off the statue enough so that it could fall if they pushed it. She called every one of the two dozen to come up and push, and when they did...the statue began swaying furiously.

All the women in the crowd outside came forth to look at the scene.

The statue began to topple and fall down. By that time, more guards in chariots had come, but only to see a fifty-foot statue falling.

And when it did fall, it left a string of dust and debris behind it. Gauri grinned, but that happiness was short-lived as guards had already come.

'What should we do now?' Mata asked.

'We need to run.'

And they did, in the opposite direction of the temple.

30

At the rendezvous point, Chandra waited for the person she was supposed to deliver the parchment to.

She had travelled close to the city of Mahishapur and it had taken a day and a half to reach there. And at the outskirts now, she hoped, things would settle. As she was waiting, she wondered about the Admiral and about how he was a good man. Better than the Devas. Or the Asuras.

He was good.

Does loss make you better? Does it give you a better perspective? It did give her perspective when she lost Bikram. But now that the Admiral had died, she had a different one.

She looked at the person entering her vicinity on his mule, a flower garland wrapped around his matted hair and a sitar in his hand that he was playing and singing. He halted the mule and got off it, walking to Chandra.

'Job well done. You are alive.'

Chandra saw the placidness in her messenger, Narada. And nodded. She handed the parchments to him. 'My mission is done.'

'Good. So you can leave for the camp in the north then,' he said, looking at the parchments. 'I'll transfer more details once you're closer to the Devas' camp from where they can then attack the treasury and loot and ransack it, so Mahisha is bled dry.'

She thought about it. All the Devas would congratulate her. But she knew she had to get back to her friends, the ones who were with her during the training program. The other four. 'I have to go somewhere else.'

Narad's expression changed. 'Where would that be?'

'I have lost plenty because of this man. I want to see that he is killed.'

'For that, there are your colleagues. They are already on it.'

'No,' Chandra sighed.

And then without turning back, she left for Mahisha.

31

Charini knew things would end badly.

But she didn't anticipate what had happened. The streets that were once littered by riotous men, had now become empty of men but now the women had come. Mahisha's statue had fallen. For inquiry and investigation, Tamar had to leave. Worse, Shukr's body was found and Tamar had to go and check if it was true or not. The people who had pushed the statue—a band of women led by her friend, Gauri—had disappeared, thankfully, and she hoped she won't be found.

Charini had also heard that Mahisha had returned from his expedition. How he reacted to the mayhem and everything—she had no clue. Charini had an idea that Shukr would be killed by Tamar, since that was what she had been hoping for, but unfortunately her plan had changed unexpectedly and both their plans had intersected, creating chaos.

Now there was no plan. She could only hope for one person to break through and kill Mahisha but...

'Was this a part of your mission?' Sulochna asked.

She knew about parts of it. But not all of it. After all, Charini had taken weeks and months to convince her, make her trust her and then tell her how Mahisha is an evil man. After Sulochna had given in to this idea, she had agreed to support Charini.

They were sitting on a cushion in the common

hall, riddled by guards and waiting for some new development.

'No...I...um...' Charini was confused. What to say?

A guard appeared.

'King Mahisha is here to see you, Lady Sulochna.'

What?

Sulochna gave a worried glance to Charini but she chided him. He had come to meet her without Tamar.

'Go. You'll be fine.'

'Accompany me?' Sulochna asked.

The guard coughed. 'Only you, Lady Sulochna.'

Sulochna nodded and pretended to be nonchalant as she followed the guard to the porch where Mahisha was waiting.

Mahisha could have come inside, but he didn't want to waste time. He was standing, grubby in the field that was there, the lawns of orchids and sunflowers, as he saw Sulochna, the beautiful, irascible wife of his friend Tamar walking towards him.

He had heard about her claims—how Tamar felt Shukr was behind her kidnapping to take over the Prime Minister's post.

And without speaking further, Mahisha had come here to make sure that she was telling the truth.

He was standing there with his new Pana soldiers guarding him. His wedding had to be stalled since unfortunately the city was not in a good position at the moment and he had to sort everything out. But before he could go in his chambers and plot out his next moves, he had to meet Sulochna.

She came meekly and bowed in front of him.

'Yes, your highness?' her head was down.

'General Seksh died,' he announced. 'I walked to the outpost and he had killed himself along with his lieutenant.'

'What? But why? That's so sad.'

'I know. Apparently Durga, this assassin, had brought strange omens to the outpost before vanishing in thin air,' Mahisha chuckled.

'Oh, I see.'

He shot her a glance. 'You know, I happen to be a very reasonable man. When I mentioned Durga to you, you didn't even flinch. Now these claims you made about guruji, I don't particularly like him, but I know he would never want to hurt his pupils. And I know you are lying.'

'N-No! I-I-I am being honest.'

He grabbed her by the throat. Tightly. He squeezed it hard. 'I should have done this earlier, but I didn't. I was stupid. And now look at me, swimming in a pool of regret. But doesn't matter, I am doing it now.'

And he twisted her neck, her form growing lifeless.

He tossed her on the ground and jumped on his stallion, ready to leave the vicinity.

Charini had seen everything, and she was screaming with horror, hidden inside, as she felt she could have saved her ally but didn't. Her face had gone white as a ghost's and she was just clinging on to…

She didn't know what she was clinging on to. She just knew Mahisha was here and it meant only one thing.

Trouble.

A few hours later, Tamar returned.

He must have heard of his wife's demise and by the time he arrived, Charini had wrapped her mistress in a white cloth and had burnt an incense stick for the foul smell to go away. She was sitting next to the corpse, while the helpless guards around the palace were in the room too.

Tamar entered and collapsed on the ground.

'I heard she was killed...killed by a rioter,' he said.

But where did he hear it from? Of course, Mahisha didn't want him to know since they were friends, perhaps. Charini grudgingly gritted her teeth as she could see him crying and beating his chest and hugging the corpse.

She remained quiet. She could do something here. Something better than she had originally planned. And this came not out of her calculations, but out of a sense of grief that she hadn't felt in a long time now. Now tears pooled in her eyes, she realised she was over this. She was over being traumatised. She wouldn't let it control her any longer. She would be tough and strong. She has to be. After all, she worked for Durga.

She leaned forward to her master who was crying and whispered in his ears, 'It was Mahisha.'

He looked up.

'Don't get alarmed. His guards are here. He has left a few around in case someone speaks out of turn or tells you something else.'

For a while, Tamar was horrified.

'There's a revolution happening, Tamar. I work with Durga,' Charini said, avoiding how she had orchestrated his wife's kidnapping since that would make him even more nervous and frustrated. 'And your king is going down. But we want your help. You are a good man.'

Tamar glanced at the grieving guards. And then back at Charini. 'You have lied...'

'Stop with your petty dramatics. Your friend has killed your wife! You should give more of a shit about her than your traitor of a friend!'

At that, he shut up. Almost crumpling with the tears. 'I can't betray my friend. I can't...even though...' he coughed, not able to say it. 'What would the Devas do to me when you win the throne?'

'They won't kill you. I promise you that,' she said. Any turned agent of the enemy would be given a second chance. At least that's what Indra had told her. 'But you have to help me.'

'And how is that?'

'Release the prisoners of war you have from the Devas' army. All the prisoners of the city,' she said. 'You are still the Prime Minister, you can do that.'

'And what good would come out of that?'

'They will side with us when the Devas enter.'

'How will they enter?'

Katya and Khushi had taken care of that. Any time now, they would be coming.

'Don't worry about that. Just do it.'

Tamar looked at Charini and then said: 'Get lost from this palace. I don't want to see your face.'

Charini could see that Tamar could take strict action against her, but he didn't. Instead, he quietly wept over the corpse of his dead wife.

And Charini, as fast as she could, came on her feet and left as she was ordered.

To rejoin the others.

32

Mahisha was frantically walking in his office, wondering how it all had begun to fall apart. Whatever he had built. Shukr was dead. Seksh was dead. And now he received the news from the messenger behind him, that the ship that was coming with a lot of gold—had exploded and had drowned. All the money was lost.

He was alone here with a messenger and the guard. But he knew Tabita and Thamisada would be coming any moment now.

'We are getting attacked left, right and centre, your highness,' the guard said. 'The outposts which were supposed to be hidden are under attack and the Deva army are infiltrating.'

I'll figure this out.

'Send the armies to the frontiers and outposts to fight back.'

'And about the treasury attacks?'

Fuck.

That too.

How did they get to know the locations?

'Send men there too.'

'But we don't have enough men, especially since there is a lot of chaos in the capital right now and people are fighting back. Ever since the statue was toppled down, the people who had blind faith in you are now turning against you,' the guard said.

'It was just a bloody statue,' Mahisha groaned.

'It was their religion and a group of people showed that it didn't exist in the first place. That it was something anyone can destroy. This broke the fear in them and they are revolting now.'

'Kill anyone who revolts then.'

Mahisha ordered him to return and relay his orders to the men, while he knew he would have to go to the frontiers now. That was his priority. Not this.

He pulled out the sack from under his table and began to gear himself up with his armour and his gauntlets and his large bullhorn helmet. As he did so, Thamisada and Tabita entered.

'What is the meaning of this?' the chief asked. 'What has happened to your city? We thought we were partnering up with—'

'You and your men are coming with me,' Mahisha cut him short, as he walked to the window to see the sight of his city. To know what had come about. 'I need your help, chief.'

Thamisada begrudgingly sighed. Tabita came and she hugged Mahisha from behind. He wasn't in the mood for love, but he agreed to the hug.

'Thank you.'

'You'll be fine,' she smiled at him.

He had treated her like shit last time, and he felt apologetic. But he couldn't just become a better person like this. He knew who he was. And he was a monster. And he would cancel the wedding once he used Thamisada in the battle.

'I need your men to fight these people,' he said to

the chief. 'The ones who are revolting.'

Thamisada nodded.

'Your highness, what is that?' Tabita asked, as she looked out of the window down at the chaos unfolding in his city.

Mahisha raised his brows as he came close to the window and saw. There were four women standing.

And he didn't know any one of them.

But one had an axe, and she had an army behind her. Dozens of people. They had already crushed the guards at his gates now. There was one with a bow and arrow, another with a sword and one wearing pure white and looking ferociously at the window.

'Who are these people?' Mahisha was confused.

And then he heard the whisper in his ears.

'Durga.'

He turned to see who was speaking.

And it was Tabita. She was coldly smiling at him.

'How...'

Thamisada came behind Mahisha and pushed him, shoving him right out of the window, and he crashed... into nothingness.

12 years back...

Shaila was trying to escape as she swam. Hard. Fast. She swam quick. She wanted to reach the shores. Her parents had been murdered and she was stuck in the icy cold water. She swam to the shore and was almost losing her body to the icy coldness, could feel her legs giving up and could feel everything...

'Hold on to this!' someone yelled.

She looked up and found her.

Her sister.

She's alive?

'Tabita?'

Her younger sister was shoving a stick at her and was telling her to grab onto it. Shaila did. And she had begun to pull herself forward, until she came to the shore.

And they hugged each other. Tabita must have hidden while Mahisha and his men were searching everything in the house.

'It'll be fine,' Tabita said, patting Shaila's head.

'It'll be fine,' Tabita said, as she walked with Thamisada and stood with the rest of the girls.

Mahisha came up on his feet, his legs weak from the long fall but he hadn't died. Far from it. He still had the energy to do enough damage. He looked in the front and saw Thamisada with the girls.

'How...' he said.

'Your men won't be able to go to the frontiers,' Tabita said, smiling. 'After all, you just voluntarily invited more than a hundred Deva soldiers who were masking as Panas into your city. You fed them and you gave them positions to fight,' she laughed.

Behind them explosions and riots wrecked the city.

Fire and fury ran through Mahishapur. It was over for Mahisha.

He turned back to see none of his guards were alive. They had all died while he was only a bit wounded from the fall.

'Thamisada...' he said.

'Well, not really...' the man pulled his helmet off and underneath Mahisha saw the blue-eyed girl. Blue eyes like ice. 'Remember me, Mahisha? You killed my parents over some milk. Well...'

Mahisha remained silent. Gulping it all down. He knew he had lost. He was a fool. The Panas...

'You were not Panas?'

'To defeat you, we became the Scythians. We conducted raids like them. We ate like them. We lived like them, just so you believed us. And then you extended your hand for our support as we knew you would since you so desperately wanted to team up with the Scythians, we took that opportunity,' Shaila was in the middle, wearing the helmet of the Panas again. She was speaking in her normal tone now and not the male voice she had used when she was pretending to be Thamisada. 'You should have caught us the day we were making you do stupid rituals. The Scythians don't even do that.'

All the women were laughing at him, mocking him. Just like that girl had when she was spying on him. She mocked him.

There was Shaila.

There was Tabita.

There was Chandra.

There was Charini.

There was Mata.

There was Gauri.

There was Katya.

There was Khushi.

There was Airavati.

All nine.

And there were others too.

He could see that the prisoners had joined too. The Deva prisoners.

And Charini was grinning for Tamar had listened. She hadn't expected that. But he had. And there were more than two hundred of them just gathered around outside Mahisha's palace.

Mahisha couldn't help but laugh at himself.

I brought it upon myself.

'It's past midnight. You couldn't kill me on the ninth night,' he was clinging on to something he could ridicule them with.

'Well, then tenth day it is,' Katya said.

He grimaced under his breath, but then he found humour in this situation, a sardonic laugh to astound his enemies, with a grin on his face.

'I have just one question,' Mahisha said. '*Who* is Durga amongst you?'

'That's the problem,' Shaila smiled, 'there was never *one* person who was Durga. We all were. Once we come together we become Durga. We are Durga. And not just us. Every woman who you have tormented. Every girl you have harassed. Every wife and every mother you have troubled. We are Durga.'

And then the rest shouted. 'We are Durga!'

They had all begun to move towards Mahisha and he pulled out his axe, ready to fight them.

And there he saw—all the nine women, they had lined up behind each other, all poised to fight Mahisha.

He noticed they all had weapons.

One was holding a sword.

Another was holding a bow and arrow.

Another was holding a mace.

In the front though, he noticed Shaila, the one he had hurt years back.

She was holding a trishul.

They all looked furious, ready to bring down anything that stood in their path. At that moment the sky parted and lightning cracked across. Somewhere a tiger roared. The sound of thunder was deafening.

'WE ARE DURGA!'

'WE ARE DURGA!'

The echoes had become louder as Mahisha's fear began to crowd over him. He could feel this was it.

It was over.

'WE ARE DURGA!'

And then he saw the weapons form a rainstorm. It came from everywhere. Searing into his flesh. He couldn't fight all of them. They stabbed him everywhere. From each end. Arrows split the air and were raining into his skull.

And he fell down. Bloody. Gruesome.

More stabs. Enough.

And when his life ebbed away, Durga continued to stab him, to fight. And they would continue to fight anyone who committed evil. For they were far stronger than any god. They were far stronger than the ones who opposed gods.

They were Durga.

EPILOGUE

It was the tenth day, early in the morning, when Narad walked freely inside Mahishapur. His men had gathered the enemies and killed them. Some became prisoners.

Narad freely moved to the main palace of Mahisha which was a sight to behold. He was waiting for this day for years now. And here it was. Right in front of him.

Crumpled and maligned and brutally butchered, there lay Mahishasura's body. All limp and dried up. And in front of him stood none other than his king—Indra—towering over him.

The priest king of thunder glanced at Narad and smiled. He had a thick white mane and bushy hair on top of his head, a white dhoti and a white shawl covering his majestic body.

Narad said, 'I believe I have come late to the party.'

'Yes, you have,' Indra chuckled. 'Though there is one problem.'

'What is it?'

'Tamar. He's alive.'

Narad nodded. 'What do you want to do?'

'I told Durga we will spare him since they wanted to do it,' he paused.

Narad didn't like the idea, but then Durga was actually a bit sentimental. 'Which brings me to this—our year-long operation has worked out.'

'Yes it has, Narad muni. But with a great grand sacrifice.'

'What do you mean?'

Indra sighed with deep frustration as he came close to the messenger and put his thick hands over his shoulder. 'The women we created, they have left.'

'We never created them, my lord,' Narad smiled at his oblivious king. 'We only gave them the weapons. They did what they were supposed to do.'

'I suppose,' he exhaled. 'And when evil strikes next, what then?'

'They will return, I'm sure,' Narad smiled.

'But they have shed that name. Durga. They said the name was only limited to the downfall of Mahisha and that it was all right for them to use it till now, but since they have left us, they don't want to continue with the name. They only killed Mahisha because *they* wanted to. Which is fine by me, I only wanted results, but it does pain me to let them go,' Indra said and coughed, as an old man would cough.

And he began to move back to his chariot which was waiting for him.

Narad had one question before his king could leave. He asked: 'If they have shed the name Durga, what name are they going by now?'

Indra turned.

'Something strange, Shaila told me,' he said. 'They call themselves...Kali.'

ACKNOWLEDGEMENTS

When a writer pens his imagination on pieces of paper, an entire army stands solidly behind him, helping him bind them into a memorable book. And I am eternally grateful to my little army for helping my voice reach the readers.

The two people I have admired most in my life: Mom and Dad, my very first sources of inspiration, without whose immense love and support this book wouldn't have seen the light of day.

Thank you to Sayantan, Megha, Rahul Sir, and the rest of the brilliant team at Simon & Schuster India for making this endeavour possible.

My agent, Anuj Sir, CEO of Red Ink Literary Agency, thank you for your priceless guidance and encouragement.

For the striking and impactful cover, a big, big thank you to team HubHawks.

Most importantly, you, the reader. Thank you from the depths of my heart for once again believing in me and picking up this book. You are amazing, and words cannot do justice to the love I have for you.

Last but certainly not the least, my inspiration for this book: thank you to all the strong and wonderful women out there for shattering the cages of patriarchy. For becoming our rays of hope in the darkness. For giving us the courage to dream.

You are heard.

To be continued...

DEVI DUOLOGY

Book 2

KALI